Praise for
The Busy Leader's Handbook

"When deciding which companies to invest in, we definitely take a long, hard look at the executive leadership team. However, it goes much deeper than that. How they develop their middle-management team is also crucial to the long-term success of a company. Sometimes, this transfer of knowledge is where companies struggle. This book is not only a great playbook for CEOs, but it would be a very effective tool for creating a strong leadership framework throughout their entire organization. It's a simple, easy read, filled with tactics that could create a strong leadership foundation in any company."

—Charles Dieveney
Managing Director
Juggernaut Capital Partners

"Quint is one of the most dynamic leaders on the planet. His new book covers all the bases on how to truly lead in a hyper-efficient world. It is an easy read that offers practical and actionable advice on how to handle almost any situation as a leader. This handbook is one that I will continue to reference and read over and over again in reflection of how I am performing as a leader. It is a book every leader should read, then go share it with their team!

"We brought Quint Studer to Springfield, Ohio, recently to help teach our leaders how to dream bigger. He humbly met with various stakeholder groups, pouring out many of the valuable nuggets shared in his new book. We are forever changed by those visits and thankful for his willingness to share with the world the tools that are now helping us build a vibrant community."

—Michael McDorman
President and CEO
The Chamber of Greater Springfield, Ohio

"Quint has hit the bulls-eye for today's busy leader! A treasure trove of fundamentals and best practices, this book goes way beyond 'ideas' and 'motivation' and delivers the 'how-to' that is so critical to every leader. This book will be a permanent resident in my briefcase for years to come."

—Brad Phelps
Owner
State Farm Insurance Agency, Pensacola, Florida

"I have had the privilege of working with Quint in various capacities over the past 25 years and can personally attest that the evidence-based practices outlined in this book can *and do* lead to astonishing performance improvements! Quint has helped me lead not one, not two, but THREE remarkable health system transformations. First, he served as my COO when I was president and CEO at Holy Cross Hospital in Chicago, Illinois. Next, he acted as a friend and advisor supporting my efforts to lead a major system turnaround during my tenure as president and CEO at Rochester General Health System in Rochester, New York. And today, he serves as a board trustee guiding the transformation work I am again leading as president and CEO at TriHealth in Cincinnati, Ohio.

"The common denominator for success in all three cases was the consistent introduction, adoption, and hardwiring of leadership, employee engagement, and organizational development practices—all underpinned by a foundation of mission, vision, and values—as outlined in this handbook. Without fail, all three organizations experienced remarkable performance improvements across key metrics, including People/Culture, Customer Experience, Quality/Safety, Growth, and Finance. And in every case, these improvements led to national recognition for being a top industry performer, and a model and benchmark for getting healthcare right.

"*The Busy Leader's Handbook* is a must-read for any leader who's short on time, but long on commitment and desire to develop great teams and organizations that are built to excel."

—Mark C. Clement
President and CEO
TriHealth

"Congrats to Quint Studer for giving it to us straight. *The Busy Leader's Handbook* is a 'must read' for anyone with aspirations to lead people and ultimately an organization.

"I loved Quint's plea for leaders to be more self-aware, to check the ego at the door, and to lead with humility. Over the years, I've seen many talented individuals sidelined by ego and/or their inability to listen.

"Successful leaders will also choose to follow Quint's blueprint for recognizing superior work while also connecting people with purpose—thus creating a positive workplace culture. Simply put, it's ALWAYS about the relationships. No matter if you are dealing with Baby Boomer, a Millennial, or someone from Gen Z—relationships will always pay.

"Lastly, I thoroughly enjoyed Quint's vision for investing in the development of structure, process, and people. A successful leader is an individual disciplined enough to set a vision and expectations while also understanding that people make the ultimate difference. It's pretty simple—great people can make great leaders.

"Again, I applaud Quint Studer for sharing his vast insights and leadership experiences. *The Busy Leader's Handbook* is a valuable tool on so many fronts."

—Dave St. Peter
President and CEO
Minnesota Twins

"Quint has now done for communities and business what he did for the healthcare community. He's identified simple, high-impact foundational leadership behaviors that, when done correctly, pack a big punch. And he doesn't just tell you the what, he also tells you the how, as the book is filled with tactics to take any leader to the next level. I believe in developing a strong leadership team and empowering them to make decisions. It can be tricky to create a team that moves in unison. A tool like *The Busy Leader's Handbook* is a great resource for training and making sure everyone is on the same page."

—Javier Hernandez-Lichtl
CEO and Chief Academic Officer
West Kendall Baptist Hospital, Baptist Health South Florida

"My life's work is to help every woman become the best version of herself. A huge part of that is focusing on the 'big picture' like passion and courage and finding your voice, but you *also* need a firm grasp of the practical side of leadership. That's what helps you connect with others in a meaningful way—and that's what *The Busy Leader's Handbook* provides. It's a practical toolkit that can help all women, including the vital group of Millennials I focus on, maximize their potential and power. I want to commend Quint's efforts and impactful work on this book, as with all his previous books. I love that he is driven to help each of us become the best we can be."

—Tiffany Pham
Founder and CEO
Mogul

"Because a few years ago I wrote a book about leadership, mentoring, and the basic laws of success, people frequently ask me about the best path to becoming a successful leader. My favorite new answer is, 'Hang around Quint Studer, and listen.' Fortunately for everyone in the pursuit of a successful leadership career or personal life, you don't have to go find Quint. He has found you.

"In his new book, *The Busy Leader's Handbook*, Quint shares a wealth of real-time, practical action steps for engaged leaders looking for answers, emerging leaders looking for an edge, and rising high achievers who want a head start. Quint addresses each of the three areas that are so very critical to a leader's success: self-leadership and self-development, employee leadership to maximize employee performance, and organizational leadership for building, driving, and sustaining a successful organization.

"*The Busy Leader's Handbook* is a reference goldmine for leaders at all levels, filled with actionable 'how-to' advice, ready to use right now and throughout a rising career.

"I wish Quint had written this book when I was 30. It would have accelerated my leadership curve dramatically and saved me a lot of scars."

—Bert Thornton
Former President and COO
Vice Chairman Emeritus
Waffle House, Inc.

"I have read a lot of leadership books over the years and this one might be my favorite. It is a simple, easy, practical read. Quint Studer has taken complex topics and broken them down in a way that makes them feel doable. (This is Quint's gift!) I also think he did a smart thing by not making this a cover-to-cover narrative—if you're struggling in a certain area you can just go to the table of contents and then flip to the needed chapter. Whether you are new to leadership or need a gentle reminder of what 'right' looks like, this is a must-read handbook for everyone in your organization."

—Ben Bates
Chairman, Coldwell Banker Ben Bates, Inc.
Chairman, Bates Hewett & Floyd Insurance Agency
Partner, Beck Chevrolet Buick GMC Dealership, Palatka, Florida

"For 15 years, my private practice as a psychotherapist concentrated on helping people work toward healthier relationships, so I naturally read *The Busy Leader's Handbook* from that perspective. Quint Studer speaks to the heart of the person, and Quint obviously understands that the best leaders are good at forging authentic connections and building relationships. Since we live in an age when these are vital business skills—they're key to creating cultures of innovation, collaboration, and engagement—this book is a must-read for anyone who leads or wants to lead. The bonus is it just might spur you on to become a better human being who doesn't shy away from all that it takes to enjoy those authentic relationships."

—Connie Bookman, LCSW
Founder and CEO
Pathways for Change

"*The Busy Leader's Handbook* is a practical, easy-to-follow 'how-to' guide for bringing out the best in yourself, your team, and your organization—and best of all, *it works!* The wisdom and proven techniques shared by Quint Studer in this book have been honed over nearly three decades of experience helping leaders and organizations achieve major cultural and organizational transformations.

"I'm a big believer in providing training and development for all my employees. At World of Beer, everyone we hire gets 40 hours of training before they set foot on the floor. We immerse everyone in our mission, vision, values, and our leadership philosophy. When I read Quint's book my first thought was 'Wow, I wish I could have gotten my hands on this when we were starting out!' I loved the simple, straightforward, practical advice. This is a blueprint for any company wanting to build a strong culture where everyone sings from the same choir book and strives to get better and better. It's a compass that ensures everyone, top to bottom, gets consistent messages about the principles of great leadership. Finally, any young entrepreneur would love Quint's insights on managing things that get in your way that you don't even know to look for—by holding up the mirror, by being humble, by staying coachable so you can adapt and adjust. My favorite part? I know Quint personally and he truly walks the walk. Highly recommended!"

—Scott Zepp
Co-Founder
World of Beer Franchising, Inc.

"My company grew from 4 employees to over 70 very quickly. Multiple layers of management sprung up between me and my frontline employees, almost overnight. Making sure everyone was living the culture wasn't easy. *The Busy Leader's Handbook* is the perfect field guide for companies going through such rapid growth. It helps you put the right structures in place—structures that help you stay focused on excellence while preserving the relationships that keep people inspired and motivated. (Walking this tightrope can be a huge challenge.) Readers will unearth lots of golden nuggets they'll want to pick up and put into practice at every stage of the journey."

—Harold Griffin, Jr.
Director of Business Development
ITL Solutions

"Before I was a small business owner, I worked in HR, so I have always been extremely interested in anything that had to do with employees. I've spent my whole career studying culture and how to create a place where great employees want to be. This book nails it! It teaches you how to create an environment where employees feel valued and cared for! It also helps you develop the kind of leaders that inspire employees to do their best and that is the absolute key to any company's success. If you can hardwire these behaviors in your organization, keeping talent in a tight labor market won't be a problem. What a great book and training tool! I wish I had written it!"

—Sondra Eoff
CEO
Odessa Pumps

"When you need to build a solid culture, middle managers hold the keys to the kingdom. We have 200 employees in seven different offices so we see this truth in action every day. Studer's book is a gold mine for this group. It's the perfect vehicle for knowledge transfer on every aspect of leadership. I appreciate that it's short and readable, almost like a streamlined encyclopedia that lets busy managers skip right to the topic they need. Like any service company, hiring the right people is huge for us and I know *The Busy Leader's Handbook* will help. I look forward to using it to select and retain talent, onboard new employees, and promote consistency in every corner of our culture."

—Drew Adams
COO
Engineered Cooling Services

"This book is a must read for everyone, especially 'Busy Leaders.' As an owner of a growing company, I encounter big and small challenges daily, and this book addressed all of them. It felt as if it had been written for me and was meant for me to read in this very moment. I also thought of every manager I work with and how the steps shared in the book are exactly what they need. Plus, the content is great and can be broken down into training segments, webinars, or seminars. *The Busy Leader's Handbook* is a business staple with tips the reader can immediately implement. Finally, I appreciate Quint's insight and how easy he makes it to apply the concepts in business. He's been a guiding light to me and our company through all the books that he's written, the seminars that he's done, and his leadership in general."

—Kristine Rushing, CIC, CPIA
COO, Risk Consultant, Beck Partners

"As a president of a Minority Chamber of Commerce, I see the *Busy Leader's Handbook* as a road map that all leaders of diverse employees should follow. Each chapter will guide leaders at ALL levels to better themselves, leverage the unique traits of their team members, and build an environment where everyone is treated fairly. Leaders often feel they can't block off long periods of time to read books, but this one is quick and easy. In fact, I could read it on my phone because it is so concise. The short chapters and repetition of key points allow leaders to quickly access the information that they need to turn today's challenges into tomorrow's opportunities. Finally, I loved Quint's emphasis on being vulnerable: it's refreshing to see a leader focus on admitting mistakes, apologizing when you are wrong, and slowing down when needed to produce desired outcomes."

—Brian Wyer
President and CEO
Gulf Coast Minority Chamber of Commerce

"This is a phenomenal resource not just for leaders and business owners, but for any person seeking ways in which to better understand how to live and interact well with others. Quint has such a talent for filtering through mountains of research and information and to deftly help us apply those important lessons in our daily lives. He delivers another well-written, straight-to-the-point guidebook for those in the field.

"As professionals are wont to do, I find myself guilty of working in the business more than on it. Just in the time it took me to read this book, I was faced with issues related to how to best conduct an employee review (there is a chapter on that), how to break down an 'us versus them' culture (there is a chapter on that), and why I tend to avoid conflict (there is a chapter on that). For a practitioner working in the business, this is a quick and fast resource for addressing the important issues of the business.

—Andrew Foxworth
Partner
Foxworth, Shepard & Bruhl, P.A.

"Reading Quint's new book, *The Busy Leader's Handbook*, was very enlightening and refreshing as I have had the unique honor of working with Quint in many different aspects. Not only is Quint training our leadership team in these exact attributes, he and his team are also working with our City Council in guiding them on the right strategic path, along with getting more civic engagement for our city.

"It is easy to get complacent as a leader when things are going well, but dealing with conflict and negativity isn't easy. This book provides great ideas and insight on making sure leaders stay focused and on the right track. A lot of the issues addressed in the book are issues the city is currently dealing with: change, employee engagement, performance reviews, and employee development and training. I will be able to take the ideas from this book and implement them to make the city of Fort Walton Beach a better place to live, work, and play, and I will be able to ensure I stay on the right track in growing as a leader along with my leadership team and all employees.

"Employees are the heartbeat of any organization. It is imperative that leaders nurture that relationship and develop employees as future leaders while making sure all employees and customers know the 'why' and the 'what.'

"This is a must-read for any leader, future leader, employee, boss, etc., as the ideas addressed in this book apply to everyone in an organization."
—Michael D. Beedie, P.E.
City Manager
City of Fort Walton Beach

THE
Busy
LEADER'S
HANDBOOK

HOW to LEAD PEOPLE
AND PLACES
THAT THRIVE

QUINT STUDER

WILEY

Cover design: Wiley

Published by John Wiley & Sons, Inc., Hoboken, New Jersey.
Published simultaneously in Canada.

For general information on our other products and services or for technical support, please contact
our Customer Care Department within the United States at (800) 762-2974, outside the United
States at (317) 572-3993 or fax (317) 572-4002.

Wiley publishes in a variety of print and electronic formats and by print-on-demand. Some material
included with standard print versions of this book may not be included in e-books or in print-on-
demand. If this book refers to media such as a CD or DVD that is not included in the version you
purchased, you may download this material at http://booksupport.wiley.com. For more information
about Wiley products, visit www.wiley.com.

ISBN 9781119576648 (Hardcover)
ISBN 9781119577317 (ePDF)
ISBN 9781119576679 (ePub)

Printed in the United States of America
V10013087_081619

To all those people who each and every day strive to help others become the very best they can be. Never underestimate the difference you make.

Contents

How to Approach This Book

Thank you for reading *The Busy Leader's Handbook.* It's meant to be a quick and easy resource for leaders at all levels. Knowing how overloaded and overwhelmed leaders can be, we purposely kept chapters short and to the point. Each one features high-impact, granular, "how to" tactics that leaders can start using right away. These tactics work. I've seen them get outstanding results over and over throughout my career.

This book has three sections. **Section 1 delves into some key leader skills and behaviors.** Together, these chapters capture the mind-set, attitude, and capabilities the best leaders tend to possess. We put them first because they are the foundation for everything else. We all need to become the best leaders we can be before we'll be able to bring out the best in others.

Section 2 is about optimizing employee performance. It explores what exceptional leaders do (and don't do) to create a positive, productive, engaging workplace culture and inspire people to consistently put forth their best efforts. Great leaders create environments in which people grow, thrive, and find a powerful sense of meaning. They lead teams in a way that creates results far greater than the sum of the individual efforts. A leader who masters these practices will set up their people to truly shine.

Finally, Section 3 addresses strategic and foundational topics. These chapters focus on the structure, processes, and groundwork that need to be in place if you're to build a successful organization. Why do we cover these last? Simply because without the efforts of leaders and employees there would be no company to run!

While it would be terrific if people read cover to cover, it's not necessary. This is a reference book and chapters are designed to be self-contained. Feel free to read the topic (or topics) you need help with in the moment and save the rest for another day. (Also, don't be surprised if you notice some crossover. Leadership is organic and its components interconnected: topics don't fall neatly into categories!)

Whether you're a new leader or a more seasoned one, I hope you will benefit from this book. Feel free to share it with other leaders and managers inside your company. The more people who embrace the proven principles of great leadership, the stronger your business will be.

I wish you and those you lead much success and fulfillment on your journeys. Leadership is a noble calling and if this book can play a small role in helping you do it better, I will be so grateful.

Quint Studer

"Wait . . . Didn't I Read This in Another Chapter?"

It would be great if you read this book straight through from beginning to end! But we know leaders are busy (it says so right in the title!) and don't always do it that way. That's why *The Busy Leader's Handbook* is written the way it is. It's set up so you can jump right to whichever chapter you need in the moment. As a result, cover-to-cover readers may find that certain tactics are repeated in more than one place.

What's more, actions that strengthen one leader's skill or behavior quite often strengthen others as well. It just works out that way. It's a good thing that so many tactics function organically to improve your leadership in several different areas: they give you more bang for your leadership buck!

Thank you for reading this book. We wish you all the best on your journey to becoming the best leader you can be.

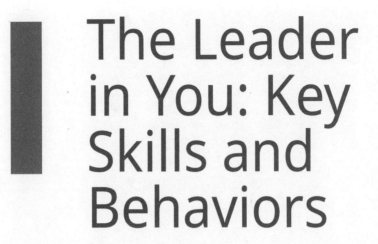

I The Leader in You: Key Skills and Behaviors

These chapters are all about the mind-set, attitude, and capabilities the best leaders possess. We all need to become the best leaders we can be before we can bring out the best in others. When we master these skills and behaviors, we lay the groundwork for a thriving organization.

1 Strive to Be Self-Aware and Coachable

Recently in a conversation with a venture capitalist, we were talking about the qualities he looks for when he is thinking about buying a company. I suspected that he would focus on things like profitability and growth potential. But to my surprise he put *self-awareness* and *coachability* in leaders at the top of the list.

I've met and worked with hundreds of leaders over the years—in hospitals, on baseball fields, in government offices, and in hotels, stores, and restaurants—and have seen what self-awareness and coachability look like in action. Organizations that encourage and nurture these two qualities in their leaders (actually, in all employees) tend to be strong, innovative, and profitable.

This should come as no surprise. Today's business environment requires us to adapt quickly and relentlessly. That means leaders must not only be great at what they do, they also have to be great learners. "They must know what they don't know"—and be willing to work hard to learn it.

Self-awareness means knowing what you're good at and what you're not. It means you don't hide your flaws or cover up your mistakes. You don't pretend to know it all. It means you practice humility and embrace learning. Not only do transparency and vulnerability help people like and trust you, they set the right example for other leaders and employees. When everyone is willing to take risks, learn from mistakes, and seek out opportunities to learn and grow, organizations thrive.

Coachability just means you're open to feedback. You don't get bent out of shape by constructive criticism. You're actually grateful for it because you want to improve and grow, personally and professionally. You want to be a better leader, spouse, partner, parent, or friend (and you know that growth impacts all of these roles).

Self-awareness and coachability are connected. Each one leads naturally to the other. When we know what we need to improve on, we're more likely to seek the help of others who can coach us. Once we seek that help we become even more self-aware. It's a cycle that builds on itself. The hardest part is getting started, but it gets easier.

When these two qualities become part of your company's culture, you're on your way to becoming an unstoppable organization. It's easier to engage and motivate employees. High performers will be drawn to you (and will be more likely to stick around). Productivity will soar.

All of this can start with one leader. By improving your own performance and setting an example for others by working to become more self-aware and coachable, you will inspire others to do the same. In fact, if you want to help others improve, this is not optional. Here is a story to illustrate what I mean:

Years ago, I was working in an alcoholism and drug addiction treatment center. I met the daughter of one of our patients, a single mom with her child's father out of their lives. This daughter was struggling in many ways, even blaming herself for her mother's drinking. I happened to know a guidance counselor at this daughter's high school who had shared with me several months earlier that she herself had grown up in an alcoholic home. I thought the guidance counselor would be a perfect person to talk to the patient's daughter.

When I called her and asked, the guidance counselor paused. She apologized, saying she could not talk to this girl because she (the guidance counselor) had not yet even addressed her own issues. For close to 30 years, this story has stuck with me. It's hard to take another person further than you take yourself.

Here are a few tips for becoming more self-aware and coachable:

Know that getting better starts on the inside. It's not "them," it's you. When I was younger I lived in the world of "if only." *If only* I had gone to this school, majored in this, grown up rich, gotten the breaks, or been more appreciated then my life would be better. The problem was always *them*. Then, at 31, I crashed emotionally. I sought professional help and found other resources to learn from. I soon discovered the problem was not *them*; it was me and my expectations. I figured out that I will struggle until I am better on the inside.

Ask for feedback (and really listen). Talk to your boss, to other leaders, to employees, to friends and family members. Ask what they see as your strengths and weaknesses. How do they think you performed on a recent project? What might you have done better?

Don't shoot the messenger. When you receive negative feedback, practice listening without reacting. If you feel yourself getting upset, don't lash out. Process the information and sit with it a while before deciding whether it's valid. Often you'll have to admit it is. It's hard to hear negative truths about ourselves but, with practice, we can become more open to it.

Have a "beginners mind-set." People who practice "beginners mind" rather than always thinking they are going to be a guru or expert tend to do better in teams. Always be ready and willing to participate, serve, and share your best insights. You will learn a lot more. For example, check your attitude before you go to a meeting. Always come into the group with the intention of learning something. Rather than having attitude of *This isn't relevant to me* or *This is not what I'm interested in,* ask yourself, *How could this apply to me? How could this be useful for me now—and if not now, later?*

Keep an accountability journal. Write down your goals and plans and regularly update what you're doing to move toward them. Track your progress over time. Are you doing what you set out to do? If not, what might be holding you back? Exploring these issues in writing can lead to startling insights on your strengths and weaknesses.

Seize every opportunity to develop yourself. While most entrepreneurs are great at the core "skill" their venture is built on—cooking, accounting, practicing law—they haven't typically mastered the skills it takes to run a business. They need training in basics like hiring, firing, creating revenue streams, etc. I find the most successful small business owners are those who are self-aware enough to know what they don't know and take advantage of resources that can help.

Hire people who are smarter than you. Make sure they're willing to challenge you (and that you're open to being challenged). Being surrounded by a bunch of "yes men" and "yes women" isn't going to help you grow.

Get a mentor, be a mentor (or do both). Jim Clifton, who is Gallup Chairman and CEO and author of *The Coming Jobs War*, writes about the need for what he calls "super mentors." He says super mentors are those who light fires under innovators and entrepreneurs and guide and advise small businesses. He calls them "the heroes America needs for this moment in history."

It's true: mentoring is powerful. Whether you have a mentor or you mentor someone else, this relationship can spark tremendous growth in both parties. Great mentors know that they are not finished products and often they learn as much from the mentee as the mentee learns from them.

Don't be afraid to change your mind. We tend to think of strong leaders as being quick, decisive, and unwavering in their decision making. Most of the time they are praised for being consistent, and their conviction seen as a source of comfort and reassurance for their team. On the other hand, leaders who change their mind or embrace a new way of thinking about something are seen as "flip floppers," and derided for being wishy-washy or inconsistent.

The reality is that leaders who are open to learning new information and adapting their thinking accordingly are ultimately more successful. Changing your mind is not a sign of weakness but a sign that you are able to learn and grow in real time. Never tie yourself too tightly to your first conclusion. Instead, have the courage to admit that you might have been wrong and the flexibility to course correct as new information becomes available. Good leaders know that new information that contradicts their current position is not a threat but an asset to be leveraged to make their plan stronger.

There is no finish line in learning. There are always things to learn. I guess I assumed at one time that someday, I would know enough. That's just not true. There is always more to learn, and teachers present themselves in many different ways. When the student is ready, the teacher appears. Remaining teachable is key.

Becoming self-aware and coachable doesn't mean striving for perfection. None of us will ever be perfect. It does mean identifying the worst flaws that hold us back and sincerely working to repair them. It means knowing which tasks to delegate, and when to seek the advice of experts. It means realizing more each day just how much we don't know.

This is a journey that we'll never finish. Our main job as a leader is to make sure that we're always headed in the right direction on the path.

2 Invite Feedback from Others and Don't Take It Personally; Instead, Take Ownership

"**D**on't take anything personally." This is the second of the Four Agreements—from the book *The Four Agreements: A Practical Guide to Personal Freedom* by Don Miguel Ruiz—that I try hard to live by. Ruiz writes that we should not take what happens around us personally because the actions of others have nothing to do with you, but rather are about them.

Although I do believe this, I also believe it does not mean we shouldn't listen to and learn from others. I recall a time when a CEO said to me that one of the senior executives had taken the low employee satisfaction results in their area personally and that she advised him not to do so. My response was they *should* take the results personally for those areas they lead. This appears confusing when considered alongside Ruiz's words.

In thinking about this paradox, I have some thoughts and suggestions:

How can we interpret results or feedback in such a way that we don't take it personally but that we learn and grow from it? Our first thought must be that the sender of the message is not trying to be hurtful but helpful. As discussed in Chapter 1, the two most vital characteristics in personal growth are self-awareness and coachability. Feedback that creates self-awareness is meant to be helpful. Having an outside perspective is valuable; remember, an artist can draw someone else better than they can draw themselves.

When we take something personally in the way that Ruiz writes about it, it can lead to unhealthy emotions, such as anger and resentment. These emotions can lead to actions that prevent one from performing a self-inventory and create situations that are unhealthy for everyone. Yes, it may feel good for a brief moment to vent, gossip, and get revenge, but rarely do these responses lead to a productive outcome.

I tend to divide people's reactions into two categories: *taking it personally* or *taking ownership of it.* The two are similar in some ways but create vastly different actions. The senior executive needs to take ownership of the poor results. What isn't helpful is blaming yourself, or beating yourself up without improving, or being upset to the point that it delays or prevents you from taking positive steps forward.

Here are a few suggestions to help you move past taking feedback personally.

1. Do a self-assessment. Is the feedback accurate? If not, is some of it right? If possible, try to find an objective measurement. Be honest with yourself. The goal is progress, not perfection.
2. If you're not sure the feedback is accurate, find someone you trust and ask them to provide a second opinion. This can be a mentor, close colleague, friend, or family member.
3. Consider where the person is coming from, their motivation, and their emotional state. Senders can have issues. An angry person may lash out, a jealous person may say negative things, etc. Take in what fits and leave the rest behind. Sadly, people can be very mean-spirited and attempt to be hurtful. By being self-aware, with the help of others, this becomes easier and easier. However, it sure is difficult at times.

   If a person is giving you negative feedback because of a past interaction with you, be aware of it but don't accept responsibility for their reaction. An example is when you hear a person say things like, "You made me angry," "You made me cry," "You made me make a mistake," "You made me happy." While we need to take ownership of our own actions, the other person must own their responses, both positive and negative.
4. Be kind to yourself. We are all human beings. Of course, when we read or hear something about ourselves or others we care about, we will be hurt. This is normal, but try to put it in perspective and

look at it as an opportunity to practice forgiveness, self-care, and hopefully the pursuit of personal growth. Don't beat yourself up or take unhealthy actions that might make the situation worse.

Make sure you're allowing people to give you feedback. I often find that leaders do not receive helpful feedback because of how they've handled it in the past. If we have reacted with silent hurt or anger, people will be reluctant to provide it again. Let the person know you will appreciate their feedback and can handle it.

Great leaders create cultures that encourage people to give feedback. Adam Grant, a Harvard professor who wrote the fantastic book *The Originals*, identified some organizations and leaders who are very successful. A common theme I noticed was that these high-performing companies had a top leader who was not only open to feedback (even when they were not in agreement), but also installed systems and behavior that created a culture where all feedback was rewarded.

This is not easy to do. Even when a leader says, "I want your feedback," many reports, due to past bad experiences, are reluctant to provide it. Some people were raised not to challenge someone in front of others and not to challenge someone in a higher position at all. In other cases, a report might say what a leader wants to hear in hopes of getting rewarded.

Creating a feedback-welcoming environment requires a leader willing to deflate their ego and be a good student. Here are a few simple tips that may help:

When someone gives you feedback in private, thank them and then ask them to bring it up in a meeting or some other public setting. When they do, thank them again, and do one better: change your position based on their feedback. This will send the message that you are open to feedback.

Ask questions. Make it very clear to those around you that you need, expect, and will appreciate their help. Use words like "Please let me know what I am missing" or "If you were going to punch holes in this and/or identify areas of concern, what would they be?" or "If you were in my position what would you be doing differently?" The key is to communicate that you are open and you need their help.

Play devil's advocate once in a while. Take a position you know has flaws and see who steps up. If someone does, thank them and recognize the value of doing so. If not, discuss the danger of group-think and ask what steps you can take to create a safe environment for feedback. Also, apologize for not having done so in the past and reiterate that you are committed to this in the future.

Use a survey tool to encourage people to give anonymous feedback. While we would love it if people felt safe to express themselves right off the bat, it takes time to create this kind of en-vironment. The use of surveys where people can respond anon-ymously can be very valuable. At our companies, we conduct an employee engagement survey each year in part to make sure our leaders are creating this kind of environment for their employees.

If you feel yourself getting emotional, hit the pause button. The more accustomed you get to receiving honest feedback, the less likely you are to take it personally. Yet we are all human, and there will be times when we *do* feel hurt or angry. When this happens, the best tool is the pause button. A bit of time can make the differ-ence between responding well and responding in a way that can make things worse. I have seldom regretted pausing. I have often regretted not doing so.

Becoming a leader who can accept feedback graciously and learn and grow from it is easier said than done. However, for you to be the best leader you can be—and for your organization to be the best *it* can be—it's critical.

Taking Ownership: Eliminating Excuses ▬

Being open to feedback is only half the battle. What matters more is what you do once a problem is pointed out to you. When we hear or discover things that we could have done better, often our first instinct is to get defensive and explain away the problem or rationalize why we made that decision. We often blame external circumstances or things outside of our control. All of this shifts responsibility away from us.

We often say things like, *How was I supposed to know? There's nothing I could have done. I was overwhelmed with other stuff. I would have, but . . .* Or, and most importantly, look out for *It's not my fault.*

These are all pretty common responses. Try to avoid these phrases (and others that shift responsibility). They aren't productive, they don't solve the problem, and they can actually be damaging in the long run. This reaction makes you seem unreliable. If you are constantly making excuses for not meeting deadlines or delivering results, it makes people feel like they can't count on you, and that hurts your credibility and career long term. It makes good people avoid working with you, as they will avoid putting themselves in a position where their success depends on you. It keeps you from fixing the real problems. When you don't see it as your fault, you probably won't make any changes, so the problem will likely happen again.

Adopt a zero-tolerance policy for excuse making for yourself and don't allow it from others. This means committing to yourself, your leaders, and everyone in the organization that you will do what it takes to get better, and take ownership of creating better outcomes in the future. This is just another way of saying that you are dedicated to doing your best work at all times, and you are focused on maximizing your impact.

When you approach your work with this mind-set, you are more likely to think creatively about how *you* might solve a problem or find an innovative work-around instead of waiting on someone or something else to make the difference. When you seek to avoid making excuses, you naturally start to think about how you can do your job better. You start to anticipate future problems, and take responsibility for outcomes. All of this will help you and your organization be more successful.

Committing to "No Excuses" doesn't mean you have to be perfect. Mistakes will happen from time to time, and are sometimes unavoidable. The difference is that you don't fall back on excuse making or avoid holding yourself accountable for improving. Instead, you actively think ahead and anticipate problems and avoid them if you can. When mistakes do happen, you take responsibility and commit to finding a way to make sure they don't happen again in the future.

When you feel yourself starting to get defensive or make an excuse, take a second to ask yourself, *Should I have seen this coming? Is there any way I could have acted differently to keep this from happening, even if no one told me to do so?* If the answer is yes, you have to own the mistake and commit to doing better moving forward.

3 To Be a Good Leader, First Learn to Be a Good Follower

Most great leaders begin their careers as great followers. They learn to *be* great leaders by *following* great leaders. And the flip side is also crucial: the best leaders know how to inspire and engage followers over the long haul. In fact, the most important quality a leader can possess is the ability to captivate, inspire, and motivate followers over time. I say "over time" because it can be easy for a charismatic leader to get followers excited about a vision once. Sustaining their willingness to follow you is a whole other ball game.

I recently shared a stage with Admiral Harry Harris, who is currently the US ambassador to South Korea. It was a great experience. It made me really think about what it means to lead and what it means to follow.

My first thought was that military leadership *must* be easier than private sector leadership because people have to do what commanders say. But then I realized it's not that easy. Not only do military leaders have unique disadvantages (for example, they can't select or deselect talent), they must build engaged followers who are in very difficult situations.

What's more, in a military or a business setting, just because people do what you say doesn't mean you'll end up with the results you want. People might "follow orders" but they can do it with half a heart and zero focus on the results. When you're a really good leader, you know how to engage people in a way that makes them *want* to follow you to the destination you've helped them see.

The mind-set and attitude of followers is very important. That's why I've come to believe that the best leaders are experts in *followership*. They understand that great leaders can't exist without great followers. It takes both roles to create a successful organization, and it's a reciprocal relationship. And the best leaders function well in both roles.

To do this it's important to acknowledge how important followers actually are. It can feel like leaders get all the glory. From all the hype you hear and read about leadership, it can seem like everyone wants to be "in charge." Of course, this is far from the truth. There are many people out there who thrive in the role of follower. They have a valuable skill they want to use and would far rather focus on applying it than spending their time strategizing, convincing, and telling others what to do. And frankly, followers can be just as valuable as leaders to the growth of a company—perhaps even more so.

The fact is, "command and control" is on its way out. Right now we are in a period of struggle as many members of the old guard still want to lead in traditional ways, while newer leaders try to figure out new models and structures that work well. As younger generations replace the older one, more change will occur. One thing's for sure: followers can no longer be passive order takers or "yes men" and "yes women." Good followership is active, dynamic, and creative. It gets noticed and rewarded.

As organizational hierarchies become flatter, followers have become more influential and powerful. It's not surprising that those who succeed at followership often transition into leadership roles later in their career.

What's more, every leader is also a follower in some capacity or some area of life. That's why everyone, whatever their title or role, needs to master the art of followership.

If you're a leader reading this I hope you will take these following tips to heart in your own work with your own supervisor. (I've found that everyone has a "boss" of some sort—even if you're the business owner or CEO, you may answer to the board of directors.) I also urge you to share them with employees as they seek to be the best followers they can be:

Bring your "A" game every day. Work ethic is one of the most critical qualities a good follower can have. I believe most people *want* to do a great job. Sometimes, though, without even realizing it, we can lose our focus. We can even get in the habit of coasting or running out the clock instead of really engaging and giving it our all. Try not to let this happen. When you're at work, really work.

Focus on intended results, not checking off boxes. Being a good follower doesn't just mean carrying out orders in a vacuum or going through the motions. It means following a vision to an intended destination. If you're not 100 percent sure what the leader wants to accomplish as a result of a task, ask them to clarify. They might just assume you are on the same page when you aren't. They will appreciate that you asked.

If you're wondering about the *why*, ask. I am talking here about the larger *why* behind what you're being asked to do. Usually, this is connected to the greater good of the customer or the company (or ideally, both). Asking about the *why* will keep you from jumping to the wrong conclusions and perhaps heading down the wrong path in order to "help." Just as important, knowing the *why* gives your work meaning and keeps you connected to a sense of purpose, which is the source of our motivation.

Always manage up the organization and the leader. Great followers know their own well-being is directly linked to the well-being of the company and its leadership. It makes no sense to tear down either, or to use "we/they" language with coworkers or customers.

Find the courage to speak up if you think the leader is making a mistake. This can be extremely tough, but part of the job of a follower is to protect the boss (even from themselves). You have an obligation to give your honest opinion. A good leader will be grateful that you care enough to give honest feedback.

If you're asked to take on more responsibility, accept it. In fact, volunteer for it when appropriate. This makes you more valuable to the company, and the experience you gain can dramatically increase your skill set. Be willing to take risks and step out of your comfort zone. You will never regret growth.

Ask for training if you don't feel qualified for something. Don't wait for the boss to offer. You are responsible for your own competency and your own advancement.

Be trustworthy. Tell the truth. Keep your word. Trust is the foundation of the leader/follower relationship, and it goes both ways. There has been a lot said and written about being a trustworthy leader, but it's just as critical for followers. The more leaders trust you, the more responsibility they'll give you and the more valuable you'll become.

Be a proactive communicator (especially with the project leader). This is so important in a complex work world with all of its moving parts. It makes you far more effective at your job. There is no way the boss can keep up with everything that's going on. Priorities can change suddenly, and by checking in regularly, you can make sure that what mattered most last week still matters this week.

Seek to be positive without being fake. Chronic complainers, naysayers, and cynics are exhausting for leaders, and they actively hurt morale. Sometimes dissent and critical feedback are necessary, of course, and it's far better to speak up than to pretend to agree with something you know to be wrong. In general, though, great followers try to create positive energy most of the time. It feels better to everyone (including you).

Strive to be a good collaborator and support your team members. If you have a best practice, share it. Step in and help coworkers when they're overwhelmed. Mentor new coworkers.

When you bring a problem, bring a solution. Great followers are problem solvers. They know the leader is probably overwhelmed and don't need one more thing dropped in their lap. Plus, as a follower, you're probably closer to the problem than the boss is and can come up with a better solution than they can. Finally, this shows ownership and contributes to a more entrepreneurial culture.

Know what the *what* is for your leader. There is probably something that really, really matters to your boss. Maybe there is one particular client whose happiness matters above all else. Or maybe they hate missed deadlines more than anything. Pay attention to your leader's *what* and laser-focus on meeting their needs in this area. They'll like you more, and you'll be able to build a productive relationship with them.

If you find that these behaviors come naturally to you, guess what? Those around you might *already* view you as a leader even if you don't think of yourself that way. Here's why.

The Best Leaders Actually See Themselves as Followers

I recently read a fascinating article in the *Harvard Business Review* written by Kim Peters and Alex Haslam.[1] In it, the authors talk about their study of Royal Marine recruits and whether they self-identify as "natural leaders" or as followers. The study found that those who viewed themselves as leaders were, indeed, more likely to be seen by their commanders as having more leadership potential than the recruits who saw themselves as followers. Yet their fellow recruits didn't agree. Peters and Haslam wrote:

> . . . we found that recruits who considered themselves to be natural leaders were not able to convince their peers that this was the case. Instead, it was the recruits who saw themselves (and were seen by commanders) as followers who ultimately emerged as leaders. In other words, it seems that those who want to lead are well served by first endeavoring to follow.

The authors write that their study "tells us a lot about the dynamics of leadership selection and helps to explain why the people who are chosen as leaders by independent selection panels often fail to deliver when they are in the thick of the group that they actually need to lead."

Here's the bottom line: in order to be perceived as leadership material, people often do things to showcase how *they* are "special" or "different." But the irony is that the best leaders are the ones who fit nicely with the group and think of themselves as followers.

I see two big lessons here for business owners and leaders:

First, when selecting leaders, choose true team players who have the capacity to form strong and meaningful relationships with employees. Choose those that give credit away.

As Peters and Haslam explain in the HBR article, elevating those who try to distance themselves from the group "encourages leaders to fall in love with their own image and to place themselves above and apart from followers. And that is the best way to get followers to fall out of love with the leader. Not only will this then undermine the leader's capacity to lead but, more importantly, it will also stifle followers' willingness to follow."

Second, if you are a leader, don't try to "seem" like a leader. Focus on teamwork and strive to create close relationships with your employees. Instead of trying to differentiate yourself, try to fit in.

We need to remember that we're *all* followers. We're all following the purpose our company exists for in the first place. Being able to do that, and do it well with people we care about, is its own reward.

No man, or woman, is an island. We all exist in relationships with other people, whether they're leaders, employers, board members, colleagues outside the company, family members, or friends. Sometimes we lead, sometimes we follow, but no matter what, we should strive to be the best human being we can be. Remember that and most of the time you'll do the right thing for all concerned.

Note

1. Kim Peters and Alex Haslam, "Research: To Be a Good Leader, Start by Being a Good Follower," *Harvard Business Review*, August 6, 2018, https://hbr.org/2018/08/research-to-be-a-good-leader-start-by-being-a-good-follower.

4 Quiet the Ego and Lead with Humility

Great leadership is not always about being "right." In fact, it rarely is. The leader's job is to bring out the best in employees and to engage them in working together to do what's best for the company. This cannot happen when a leader is too attached to their own ideas or convinced that they are the smartest person in the room. That's why humility is one of the most important traits a leader can have.

Let's start by getting past the notion that humility is about being meek or submissive or thinking you aren't good enough. It's none of these things. We can take pride in our work and have confidence in abilities and *also* be humble. Humility is about seeing oneself as one truly is. We know our strengths and our weaknesses. When we're good at something and we receive a compliment, we don't deny it. When we make light of our skills it can make others feel bad. Rather, we're grateful that we're in a position to help others develop that strength.

Leading with humility is about taking oneself out of the center of the equation, about keeping the spotlight on others. It's about quieting the ego so we're open to learning and we're focused on continuous improvement and growth.

Humble leaders don't assume they have all the answers. They know that an inflated ego can cause them to make bad decisions and lead the team down the wrong path. Also, it can alienate employees rather than engaging them, create dependency rather than ownership, and promote individualism rather than teamwork. It can also send the wrong message about learning—which is especially dangerous in a time when learning is the key to survival.

In a global economy where everything changes rapidly— marketplaces, competitors, consumer behavior, technology, etc.— organizations must be able to quickly shift in response. They must be great at innovating, problem solving, and practicing all the other soft skills that are so important and valued. An openness to learn-ing (in fact, a love of learning) is at the heart of all of this—and humility is at the heart of *that.*

In this arena, as in others, leaders must set the example for every-one else. When they're constantly questioning and seeking new per-spectives, new knowledge, and better ways to do things, others will follow their lead. Collaboration, teamwork, and innovation flow from there. This commitment to continuous learning is how your company gets better and better.

So what does humility look like in action? For starters, humble leaders are those who direct their focus outward. This gives them a situational awareness that serves the company well. When we inten-tionally focus on other people, we notice things we might not have seen otherwise. We pick up on body language and subtext. This allows us to see things others miss and helps us build stronger relationships.

Leading with humility means we don't mind seeking the input of others before making decisions. This allows us to harness the intelli-gence of the entire team. In an incredibly complex world there is no way one person can know it all.

It means we never push our self-interest over that of the group. We make hard decisions with everyone's needs in mind, not just our own. We know that a rising tide lifts all boats.

Also, leading with humility means we don't mind asking for help. And because humble leaders are well-liked and appreciated, we will receive it. People are much more likely to help those who don't come across as know-it-alls or showoffs.

First, Diagnose: Do You Have a Humility Problem?

The first step to getting better is always being aware that one has a problem. Hold up the mirror and ask yourself a few questions:

- Are you constantly reminding the people around you of how great or talented you are? Your ability should be evident in the work that you do. People will notice, and your credibility will come about organically.

- Are you concerned with what you "deserve"? Do you feel you should get special treatment because of your position or abilities?
- Do you find yourself name dropping, or talking about who you know to feel important?
- Do you require a lot of positive reinforcement? For instance, do you point out your own shortcomings as a way to fish for reassurance, or do you reject compliments when people offer them? When you know your own value, you don't need to do this.
- Are you a perfectionist? Do you overreact to others' mistakes? These can signal a lack of humility because they imply that you believe you try harder than (and are better than) everyone else.
- Are you self-righteous? Do you find yourself judging others (often openly) and talking about how you would never do the things they do?
- Do you take credit for things that were actually a team effort?
- Do you feel that menial tasks are beneath you?
- Are you inflexible, exhibiting a "my way or the highway" mentality?
- What are your motives? Do you go above and beyond because you value success of the organization, or do you do it to gain affirmation?

These questions can help you become aware of any red flags that may signal a lack of humility. Hopefully, very few of them apply to you, but most of us have humility slip-ups from time to time. The key is to be aware of it and rein in the ego when it starts getting out of control.

When we get intentional and proactive about leading with humility we will naturally shift to a healthier state of mind. The ego will assert itself less and less. Here are a few tips:

Always model what you want to see others do. Never ask your team to do anything you aren't willing to do, or expect them to keep standards you yourself aren't able or willing to keep. Humility means knowing everyone stands on level ground. Leaders don't try to present themselves as "special" or "different." (See Chapter 3.)

Develop and promote others on the team. If you find yourself keeping things for yourself to do to show value, you are likely not coming from a place of humility. A humble leader will eventually render themselves obsolete in their current role, and then move up! Transfer ownership; raise your team up.

Give others credit. Push compliments down to the team. Actively look for places where you can give someone else the win—even better if it's a junior person and you can use the opportunity as a learning experience. This means teeing them up nicely to be able to deliver something, then recognizing them for doing a good job.

Be accessible. Don't lock yourself in your office. Leading with humility means getting down in the nitty-gritty with the team. Work with them, spend time with them, try hard not to be aloof or unapproachable. Make it clear that you have time for them and value interacting with them.

Know when it's appropriate to micromanage. On one hand, humility means letting go of doing things "our way." If someone finds a new or better way of doing things, rejoice! We've done our job and helped them grow. On the other, we need to know when to micromanage. If we take a totally hands-off approach we may set an employee up to fail. Then, we get to swoop in and be the hero. This is self-serving and the opposite of humility.

Strive to be coachable. Seek to be a learner above all else. Be curious, ask if you don't know. Don't be afraid to admit if you don't understand or don't know what to do. Even the best leaders have strengths and weaknesses, and they never forget this. Ask questions as much as you can. Make a point to learn something from everyone on the team. This helps you keep your focus on them (and off yourself) and helps you recognize some of their abilities you might not have otherwise noticed.

Seek input and feedback regularly, and make sure people feel "safe" enough to tell you the truth. Whether you're getting the team's perspective on a decision you're trying to make, or asking how things are going with their jobs (and your leadership) in general, it's important to foster a culture of psychological safety. (See Chapter 21.) Leading with humility means always seeking out the truth, especially if it's something you might not really want to hear.

Don't focus on who the other person is or where they fall in the hierarchy. Focus on what they're saying and whether it is true. A humble leader can take feedback from every level of the organization. If you find yourself saying, "They're not the boss of me" (or something along those lines), you might be coming from a place of pride rather than humility.

Speak the truth for the right reasons. Be authentic. Don't sugar-coat, or package things in a way to try to make yourself look better. When you have to break hard news to someone, do it from the right place. Don't make them feel or look bad if you don't have to. Don't make a huge production out of calling someone out, or use it as an opportunity to signal your own virtues.

Listen to understand, rather than respond. Communication should always be a two-way street. In a conversation, really try to empathize and understand what the other person is saying. This will help you get a better picture of what their needs or concerns really are. You should always be thinking "How can I help this person?" or "How can I make things better?"

Admit mistakes. Don't be blinded by pride or try to portray yourself as perfect. People appreciate vulnerability in leaders. Apologize sincerely when you need to. Remember the three magic words to reset any relationship: *I was wrong.*

Be open and transparent. Share information when you can. Don't keep secrets, or withhold information just because it came to you first. This can make you feel more powerful, but it only damages the group. Sometimes you might have to keep information under wraps for a specific reason, but have good judgment as to when that really matters versus when it is just driven by ego.

Look for ways to make others feel important. A wise man once said: "When I talk to a boss, I get the feeling that they are important. When I talk to a leader, I get the feeling that I am important." When someone does something well or makes a critical contribution to a project, say so (if you can do so publicly, so much the better). This shouldn't be hard to find: everyone has gifts they bring to the table and the humble leader strives to be always on the lookout for them.

Don't talk about where you are, talk about who helped you get there. (Know your own privilege.) Be appreciative of the opportunities and "breaks" you got along the way. There is no such thing as a leader who got to the top on their own. Even when you talk about your own success, make the focus on who helped get you there, not how great you are.

Don't put yourself down or deny compliments. Part of humility is knowing that you're good enough, and basing your self-worth on your own assessment of your performance. Be aware of "false" humility, which is putting yourself down so that others rush in to affirm how great you are. Also, when someone pays you a compliment, don't deny it. If someone says, "You're a really great speaker," don't say, "Oh, it's nothing." This may make the person feel bad because *they* don't have that skill. Then they will be less inclined to ask you for help, which means you lose a chance to serve them. It's better to simply say "Thank you. I work very hard at it."

Likewise, don't be a martyr or seek pity from others. The "poor little old me" mind-set is the opposite of humility. If you want people to feel bad for you, you are still sucking up all the attention and focusing it on yourself.

Say thank you at every opportunity. Recognize team members who contributed to the success. This is a good exercise in focusing on others, not yourself. Seek to always lead (and live) from a place of gratitude. In a way, gratitude is the ultimate marker of humility. I've heard it said that EGO stands for "Edging God Out." Being grateful is a way of acknowledging that our gifts come from a Higher Power—and even those who aren't religious in the traditional sense will benefit from acknowledging that they aren't the source of all good things.

Leading with humility is not easy. It actually requires more self-assuredness and confidence than leading with arrogance and ego. We owe it to ourselves and others to do the work to develop this inner strength. When we do, we won't need the external reinforcement that leads us to put on a show and seek accolades. We'll be the kind of leader that others trust and follow.

5 Let Values Be Your Guide

Roy E. Disney was quoted as saying, "It's not hard to make decisions when you know what your values are." To me this quote sums up why every leader must have a deep understanding of their company's values, commit to live by them, and convey them to employees. Every day leaders and employees make one decision after another on behalf of the company. Something needs to guide those decisions. That "something" is *values*. They are your company's compass.

Values tell everyone how to behave—what to do, what not to do, and where the boundaries are. When everyone clearly understands and agrees to live by a set of values, it pushes decision making downward. Employees know what the rules are. Everyone speaks to customers in a unified voice. All of this promotes alignment and consistency. In the end, the company enjoys better performance.

In his book *Built to Last*, Jim Collins examined companies that last a long time compared with those that do not. The research showed that values play a critical role in organizations that are able to attain and sustain success.

Values go a long way toward shaping and sustaining a strong company culture. They have a major influence on a person's behavior and attitude and serve as broad guidelines in all situations. I have found that once an outcome or behavior is connected to values, a person will follow through even if it makes them uncomfortable. After doing the behavior for a while, what was uncomfortable becomes comfortable.

For example, let's say an employee left it to the last minute to order material and had to pay extra shipping, or did not take the time to research the most cost-effective product or material and ended up spending more than needed. A value of the company is financial stewardship, and you explain that not using resources as well as possible puts the company at risk. When the employee hears it explained this way, they will plan more carefully in the future.

It is a leader's job to hardwire a strong set of values into the organization. Here's how:

1. **If you already have a strong set of company values, ask yourself how well you are communicating these and connecting staff actions to them.** Review them, make sure you they are current, and if need be, revise them. (See Chapter 30 to learn more about how values work in conjunction with mission and vision.) Be aware that while most companies do have written values, often in employee surveys the question "my company lives the values" is rated low. The idea is not merely to have them "posted" but to repeat and refer to them often enough that people integrate them into their own value system. As I once heard someone say, values don't just hang on the walls, they walk in the halls.

2. **If you do not have a strong set of written values, create them.** Go online and look up "workplace values" and you will find many lists of example values. See which five or six best fit your department or company. Here are a few examples of some common corporate values and how leaders might live them:

Transparent

- Communicate what is going on, especially with sensitive or controversial topics.
- Narrate the "why" behind decisions. When people understand why, they are more likely to agree.
- Live by the sunshine rule: keep everything out in the open, even if it's not popular.
- Don't have a meeting before the meeting.

Innovative

- Have a system for collecting fresh ideas. Ask people to share, and really listen to them. (Maybe ask people to contribute a new idea every month.)

- Reward and recognize people who engage in the innovative process.
- Be open and willing to change and progress.
- Don't demonize failure.

Focused

- Plan the work and work the plan.
- Pick a few things that will make a difference and commit to doing them really well.
- Don't get distracted by every shiny ball that rolls by.
- Put all of your attention and resources behind the projects you can really impact.

Resourceful

- Creatively look at the resources you have access to and use them in the most productive way possible.
- Tap in to resources that might usually go overlooked.
- This might mean identifying new resources you didn't realize you had, or thinking differently about the resources already available.

Team-Oriented

- Be a "bridge builder": actively look for ways to connect with other stakeholders.
- Create opportunities to help each other make things better for everyone.
- Coordination between many moving parts.
- Groups at every level working toward a shared vision or end point. Find projects they can partner on.

Accountable

- Do what you're supposed to be doing, when you're supposed to be doing it.
- Make judicious decisions that weigh all factors.
- Set reasonable goals that everyone agrees on, and enforce them.
- Meet deadlines and make sure others do, too.

3. **Write the values down and make sure people know what they mean.** Operationalize them so that people know what right looks like. Let's take the last example from list above—*accountable*—and bring it to life. Here's how employees might live this value:

   ■ Do what you say you're going to do. If you're not sure you can do it, don't promise it. Overpromising and overcommitting ensures that you'll drop the ball at some point.

   ■ Keep your appointments. Everyone has to reschedule sometimes, but make it the exception, not the rule.

   ■ Be on time for work and for appointments. In fact, strive to be a few minutes early.

   ■ Be scrupulously honest. Don't tell little white lies. They have a way of growing bigger and bigger and eventually you will be found out.

   ■ When you screw up, admit it. Don't make excuses.

   ■ Don't assign blame and point fingers. Instead, look for ways you can be part of the solution.

   ■ Follow up with team members to make sure projects aren't falling through the cracks. Don't just say, "Oh, well, I did my part."

   ■ If you need to work late to get it done, work late without complaining. There are also days you leave early. It all balances out in the end.

   ■ If you're out of something to do, ask for more work. Don't wait for someone else to direct you.

   By spelling out exactly what the values look like in action, you go a long way toward making sure people are living them. People generally want to do a good job, giving them a roadmap will set you both up for success.

4. **Make the values very visible to all employees.** This is also true of your mission and vision statements. Post them prominently throughout your company. Include them in standards of behavior (see Chapter 32), emphasize them when you hire, reference them when you train a new skill, reinforce them in meetings, and so forth.

5. **Connect to values on a regular basis.** In written and verbal communication, connect back to values. For example:

   "Susan, I saw how even though you were busy, you took time to help your coworker. This is a great example of living our value of teamwork."

"Adam, I know getting the customer feedback you received was not pleasant; however, I noticed you were not defensive and took positive action. You really role-modeled our value of learning."

Always add a sentence to what you write or say with a connection to values.

6. **Don't ignore violations when you see them.** Remember, *what you permit, you promote.* When addressing people who are not taking the desired action, connect it to not living the company values. If values violations keep happening, you might find you need to put new systems in place (perhaps a better performance management process) to tackle the issue and make sure you're not permitting/promoting it. Encourage employees to do the same.

7. **Hold up the mirror.** As a leader, you are always being watched. Are you demonstrating the values? An employee of an organization once asked me what to do if your boss is not living the values. I asked for more information. He shared that everyone was supposed to wear their name badge near their left shoulder. Yet the top leader never wore his name badge. I suggested he bring this up to the leader, but he was uncomfortable doing so. So when I saw the leader I mentioned that an employee had shared he felt he was not being consistent. The leader stated: "While I wish he would come to me, he is right and from now on I will wear my name badge." I suggested he let everyone know this subject had come up, thank people for bringing it to his attention, and ask that if they notice other things to please speak up.

Occasionally, whether you're a leader or an employee, you may be asked to do something that goes against company values. This is a challenging situation. However, it's exactly in times like these that values are the most critical. How you respond will demonstrate whether you are truly living the values. Here are some guidelines to follow in such a situation:

What to Do When Asked to Go Against Values

1. When asked to do something that is not correct, explain to the person asking you to take the action why you feel the way you do. This gives the person the chance to share information that you may not have.

2. If after getting the explanation you are still uncomfortable, explain why and offer to talk with others in the company if need be.
3. Document conversations.
4. If you see action that is not correct and your direct supervisor is not listening, go over their head. Many companies even have hotlines today.
5. If there is retribution in response to your actions, report it.
6. If necessary, reach out to state and national hotlines. Also seek legal advice.

Hopefully, the values your company publicly claims are positive, ethical, morally correct ones. Most are. And hopefully those company values match your own personal core values. I find that the best leaders are those who embrace the same set of values both on and off the clock. They are transparent, or resourceful, or accountable at work *and* at home and in the community.

I have heard it said that character means you do the right thing when no one is looking. I absolutely agree. It is often hard to do the right thing—to make the right values-based decision—but it is worth it. And you only think no one is looking: most times, someone is. Walk the talk always. You'll be able to look at yourself in the mirror and look your children, partner, and friends in the eye and you'll guide your employees to do the same. That's great leadership.

6 Be a Good Communicator

Great leaders are almost always great communicators. They have to be. Leaders must not only share information with many groups—employees, managers, customers, investors—but deliver it in a way that motivates people to act. That means knowing how to communicate in such a way that each audience truly "hears" the message, is inspired by it, and is willing to work hard toward common goals. This is a real art form.

Great communication is not just about people understanding what you are trying to say. It's also about how they react to it and how they feel about you afterward. You want people not just to hear what you say but also engage emotionally with it. When they take your messages to heart and move enthusiastically toward the goals you've set for them, you know you've been successful.

Being a great communicator is more important than it has ever been. For one thing, the world is noisier than ever before. It's hard to get people's attention. It's the digital age, so messages fly at people from all directions. Leaders need to be able to break through the chaos and say what they need to say in a way that will truly be heard and paid attention to.

As work environments are extremely complex and overflowing with information, part of being a good leader is managing the flow. Leaders need to be able to make sense of all this information and manage it in a way that gets everyone aligned and on the same page, keeps teams from getting siloed, and keeps everyone from feeling overwhelmed.

This is certainly not easy. For example, consider that more and more folks are working remotely. Even those who go into an office spend most of their time behind their desk and plugged into a computer, so there are fewer opportunities for chance encounters or face-to-face interactions between coworkers.

It just takes a much more intentional approach to keep everyone connected and on the same page. There may be things others need to know that you might not think about looping them in on, or vice versa, or bright spots that should be leveraged but could easily go unnoticed.

In an increasingly team-oriented and collaborative world, leaders must be ready and able to send, receive, and pass along massive amounts of information. Whereas in the past a person might be a part of one or two teams, today they're often expected to be part of many different projects and to move effortlessly between them. That means we *must* have good communication habits in place. We can't literally be in two places at once (at least until we figure out cloning), but good communication can help you stay connected to more than one place at a time.

Finally, leaders must be able to build strong relationships. They are the foundation for everything else. Leaders must communicate in ways that nurture and enhance relationships. Great communication from leaders sets people up to do their best work, helps them improve and grow, and connects them to a sense of meaning and purpose. If you can do all of these things you will automatically create healthy, mutually beneficial relationships.

All of that said, what does great communication look like in action? Here are a few tips for communicating well and making sure the rest of your team does so, too:

You have to walk the walk *before* you can talk the talk. First and foremost, being a great communicator must be underpinned by reputation. It's not just about mastering the technical aspects of communication, it's about doing great work. It's about being credible. When you are solid, honest, and authentic, people will trust you and be receptive to what you have to say. This is more than half the battle.

Practice being a great listener. This is a fundamental part of being a great communicator. Learn to listen actively. Give the person speaking your full attention. Rather than calculating your response while the other person is talking, try to stay focused on understanding what they're saying. It can help to ask an occasional question or make a comment that shows you're following what they're saying.

Finally, summarize what you heard in order to confirm that what you think they said is actually what they meant.

Make communication a regular part of your job. Don't communicate only when you think there is "news." People need to know what's going on in an organization at all times. Even if you assume they know certain things, there's a good chance they don't. It can be tempting to deliver only good news. Yet visibility and communication are even more important when things are tough. People imagine the worst and this can create anxiety.

Carry your own messages to employees and to other senior leaders. People want to hear from their leaders directly, especially on sensitive issues. It's important to face employees to say what you think and not deflect or rely on higher-ups to share bad news. Likewise, your boss wants to hear from you directly and will respect you for reaching out with any concerns. When you carry your own messages you model this behavior for employees and they will be more likely to do the same. This is a key component of ownership.

Choose your method wisely. Know when to email, when to call, when to show up in person. Face time (*real* face time, not the kind that happens on your smart phone or computer) counts for a lot. When you can't be face to face, know what should be said in an email and which conversations will require a phone call. Sensitive topics should definitely be addressed face to face or at least over the phone. So should those that have a lot of confusing details where people will need to ask questions (it's just so much more efficient than a lot of back-and-forth emails).

Know that communication is more than just the words you say; it's all the things that go alongside that. Human beings are hardwired to read and respond to tonality and nonverbal cues. Make sure you're aware at all times what you're projecting to others. Pay attention to:

- Tone. The way you say things matters. Does your voice sound strong and confident or anxious and hesitant? Optimistic or worried?
- Body language. Think about your facial expressions and posture, but also about how you're standing (or sitting), whether your arms are defensively crossed or relaxed, etc.
- Timing. When you deliver a message is just as important as the message itself, and makes a huge impact on how people

respond to it. If you have to send a tough email or deliver a tough message, think about when best to send it.

- Setting. Being visible, and face to face, as much as possible helps build credibility and allows you to create a more personal relationship. Also, where are you physically located? Are you trying to stop someone in a hallway with a long, drawn-out discussion? Are you having a private conversation in a public space? Pay attention to where your employees will best receive the information that you put out. If no one looks at the bulletin board, it probably isn't the best place to put critical announcements.

Be clear and simple with your messages. Try to eliminate all traces of vagueness. Make it obvious: this is the goal, this is how long the task will take, these are the resources you'll need, here's how you can streamline the process. People just respond better to simplicity, and if you aren't absolutely clear you'll just have to explain it again later (possibly after they've done it the wrong way).

Tailor messages to the audience. Don't say it the same way in the board room that you'd say it in the machine shop. Good communication means being able to speak the same language as your audience. (Even so, there's no reason to "fancy things up" for C-suiters, board members, or high-level clients. Most people appreciate simplicity and plain language.)

Be as transparent as possible. We talk about this elsewhere in the book, but it bears repeating here: be as transparent as you can be at all times. When people feel you have a hidden agenda, they don't trust you and they are likely to feel anxious. If there is a valid reason why you can't tell them everything, just say so. Otherwise they will read this as you being evasive. Be honest in good times and in bad.

Use communication as an anxiety-relieving tool. Keep people posted on projects that are underway. If an important deadline is coming up, regularly check in with both higher-ups and employees and let them know, "Hey, we're in good shape." When you know an issue or event is on someone's mind, be proactive about keeping them in the loop. When they hear nothing, people tend to assume the worst. The more you check in, the less anxious they'll be. Always seek to demystify and reassure with regular communication.

Don't bombard people with too much information. If you're constantly talking and sending a thousand emails, people will tune you out. Make sure they truly need the information. Make good decisions about who you copy on emails. Literally say, "If I am copying you and you don't need to be copied please tell me." Never use a blind "cc." Also, don't overload their inbox over the weekend. They'll only feel overwhelmed and dread Monday morning.

Constantly ask yourself, "What do I know that others might also need to know?" The irony is that while people complain about too many meetings and too much email, they also feel they aren't getting the information they really need. Always be thinking about what you need to share with people so they can do their job to the best of their ability.

Communicate important things more than once and in a variety of ways. If it's a critical message you may want to say it 10 different ways: in meetings, in emails, in company newsletters, in routine conversations about projects. Remember, your message has to get through a wall of information so it's better to err on the side of saying it too many times versus taking the risk of not being heard. Also, know people's preferred communication methods—some prefer email, some prefer phone calls, some prefer a face-to- face meeting—and use them when you can.

Be sensitive to making virtual workers feel part of the team and "in the loop." In other words, Skype or videoconference whenever you can. It's easy for these workers to feel cut off from the rest of the company. Seeing your face on their screen will help. On the rare occasions when you do get to see a remote employee face to face, really make the most of it. Try to do something fun. You will send the message that they're a key part of the team and you genuinely care about them.

Don't assume people are hearing what you say. Verify by asking if they understand. Communication is a two-way street. Be sure employees respond to you in a way that lets you know they truly "heard" what you said. (As mentioned earlier, this is part of being an active listener.) The way you communicate as a leader sets the example, but if they aren't picking up on it don't hesitate to say so. Also, narrate the importance of good communication practices so they will adopt them, too.

Regularly communicate bright spots and wins. This is the kind of communication that feels good to leaders and employees. It doesn't always come naturally to leaders because we are trained to look for problems and solve them, but we need to share positive messages often. Research shows it takes a 3-to-1 ratio—three positive messages for every negative message—for people to feel good about you as a person and a leader. Get intentional about sending these kinds of messages.

Make good communication part of your culture. Make sure you're sending the right messages about valuing communication. Be easy to communicate with. Keep your door open and make sure people know they are welcome to talk to you at any time. When they come to you with an issue, be welcoming and ultra-responsive. Encourage people to ask questions until they understand; don't make them feel like they are interrupting or irritating you.

Also, put systems in place to make sure people "get" the importance of regular communication. For example, tell them to send their to-do list several times a week so you know exactly what they are working on. You might also want to set aside a few hours at least once a week for employees to connect on a deeper level. During this time they can approach you with any concerns or questions they may have. This will train you and them to make time for focusing on communication.

Communication is how work gets done. *Great* communication is a force multiplier. It makes everything you do more effective.

When you zero in on how well you are communicating and really get intentional about doing it better, you will be amazed by how much improvement you'll see. You may find that there are fewer mistakes and that people meet their deadlines more often. You may find that, in general, there is less anxiety, more engagement, and a more positive culture. Not a bad payoff for paying attention to the messages you're sending.

7

Know How to Get Things Done:

Hit the Brakes on the Ideas; Hit the Gas on the Execution

Have you ever come out of a brainstorming meeting all pumped up about all the great ideas, only to realize later that none of them came to fruition?

Most companies have no shortage of great ideas, and great ideas *are* important. Innovation is valuable. It keeps us sharp and competitive. Besides, it's easy and fun to get excited about big ideas. What's not quite so sexy is executing them. And so, too often, these companies just don't.

A tendency to fall short on execution creates serious challenges for a company. In a business world that gets more complex and moves faster every day, being able to execute quickly and efficiently is a survival skill. Competitors are everywhere and customers have extremely high expectations. The organizations that perform well in this high-pressure environment are those whose leaders have a bias toward execution. It's not that they discourage innovative thinking. It's that they know how to put boundaries around it and operationalize it.

When big ideas are flowing fast and furious, trying to process them all is like drinking from a fire hose. People get so overwhelmed that they can't take in everything and they can't move ahead on anything. (This is especially true in small companies, where everyone is so busy just running the day-to-day business that there's little time for anything else.) They end up going a mile wide and an inch deep on things instead of picking a few items and doing them really well.

My experience has been that the organization that can take one or two ideas and relentlessly work to bring them to fruition will be far more successful than the group with a million great ideas.

This can be confusing to employees. Naturally everyone believes their boss wants to hear great ideas. I just heard an interesting story about a new chief marketing officer who was having trouble with the CEO. At the heart of the matter was all her great ideas (believe it or not). What the CEO really wanted was someone who could execute the basics the former CMO wasn't able to get done (like creating a new website).

Ideas matter, but execution matters more. I always tell companies to hit the brakes on the ideas and hit the gas on execution. This doesn't mean giving up on big ideas altogether. It means being more thoughtful about which ones you pursue, then giving the vast majority of your focus to executing on them. A few tips that may be helpful:

Benchmark others. If someone has already solved the problem there's no need to reinvent the wheel. Some years ago, I read an article in the *Harvard Business Review* entitled "Imitation is More Valuable Than Innovation." Author Oded Shenkar pointed out that almost 98 percent of the value of innovations actually goes to those who imitate them.[1] Don't think you have to be first to market. You can save valuable time and resources just by making it a habit to learn from others.

Train yourself to notice and seize opportunities. Successful leaders are good at spotting opportunities and acting on them. Often when we think of seizing opportunity we tend to envision big-picture, game-changing kinds of events. We end up overlooking the smaller, everyday chances to make something better. (Quite often, the most valuable opportunities present themselves as problems.) You might think that these little things don't make a difference, but the cumulative effect of a lot of little things has a huge impact over time, not to mention these smaller things are often much easier to execute and maximize.

Seek consent, not consensus. When seeking to act on a new opportunity, we usually need to move quickly and efficiently. This means that, quite often, we don't have time to change everyone's mind before we act. We can't seek consensus in our decision making. We must seek *consent* instead. While it's good (and necessary) to collect input from people inside the organization, when we try to please everyone, we just get mired down and nothing happens.

There will always be resistance. However, when you consistently treat people with respect, transparency, fairness, and gratitude, you increase the likelihood that they'll accept your decision—even if they personally disagree with it.

Pick a few big ideas that you want to pursue. Begin with two or three only. No company can focus on too many things at once. You want a maximum amount of brainpower and energy directed at a few, very crucial projects, rather than having it divided up thinly among too many.

Think carefully about sequencing. Which big idea should come first? Often there is a good reason to put Idea 1 ahead of Idea 2. Think it through before you set the project in motion. (However, don't fall victim to analysis paralysis or wait for conditions to be perfect. At some point you just have to pull into traffic.)

Do the same kind of thinking after you've selected a project and are ready to get started. Like building a house, executing an idea requires that you do things in the right order. Try to do too many things at once (or in an order that doesn't make sense) and the project gets too complicated and stalls out.

Think about the organization's priorities and the timing. A good idea at the wrong time can turn into a bad one quickly.

Build in some small wins to get momentum going. Start with an easy target goal that helps you make progress on your first big idea. This builds up people's confidence and enthusiasm. Small wins lead to bigger wins, which lead to even bigger wins.

Know who your drivers are. There are some people who just know how to get things done. You probably know right away who these people are inside your company. Make sure they are leading the projects.

Tie performance reviews to getting things done. Rewarding and recognizing outcomes (not just raw ideas) sends the message that execution matters more than a lot of talk about what "could" be. Set clear, objective, measurable goals for the project leaders and weight them in a way that clearly shows that execution is a top priority. When people know they will be graded (and compensated) on something, they are far more likely to do it than if they are given some vague, open-ended assignment.

Hold regular meetings to ensure that progress is being made. These "check-ins" not only reassure you that your big ideas are being executed, they keep project leaders focused and motivated. They force people to show progress. Plus, they give you a chance to course-correct early if it turns out something isn't working like you thought it would.

Don't get hung up on perfection. Trying to get things perfect slows down and, in some cases, prevents execution. It causes people to miss deadlines and to spend too much time trying to polish up a project when they really should be moving on to the next one. I have always found that most of the time 90 percent is good enough. It's when you're obsessed with getting to 100 percent that your momentum slows and you may even stall out.

Celebrate milestones along the way. Spotlighting progress helps build momentum, and enjoying regular success is important for creating meaningful work and keeping employees engaged and satisfied.

Having a process in place to help people execute ideas is crucial. When your company has a lot of big ideas that don't get off the ground, people get cynical. They don't believe anything is really going to change. This kind of cynicism can really drag down the culture.

On the other hand, when you have a big win, people gain confidence. They get excited about the next idea. They get motivated to bring it to life. This energy and enthusiasm become part of your culture, and, before you know it, a focus on execution is part of your company's DNA. This is when things really take off—and you're well on your way to being a perpetually high-performing organization.

Note

1. Oded Shenkar, "Defend Your Research: Imitation Is More Valuable Than Innovation," *Harvard Business Review*, April 2010, https://hbr .org/2010/04/defend-your-research-imitation-is-more-valuable-than -innovation.

8 Get Intentional About Time Management

The ability to get things done is the hallmark of a great leader. How well do you, the individual leader, execute day by day? Do you meet deadlines? Do you move projects forward quickly or are you a bottleneck? Do you give most of your focus to the most important things—or do you frequently let meaningless tasks eat up your day?

What we're really talking about here is time management. The scarcest resource for any leader is time. We have 24 hours a day, we spend maybe 8 to 12 of those at work, and it's how we put those hours to use that determines what kind of leader we are—not to mention what kind of parent, spouse, partner, and friend. We need to get intentional about time management practices if we are to break the (sometimes unconscious) habits that are holding us back.

Great time managers are usually better leaders. Obviously, they are more productive. They make fewer mistakes and have to do less rework. (It reminds me of a saying I heard somewhere: *If you don't have time to do it right the first time, you don't have time to fix it!*) They are able to spend more time on learning, strategizing, and being well prepared—which creates more opportunities. And, of course, they get to spend more time coaching and mentoring—which helps employees become higher performers—which helps the company thrive.

The good news is that time management is a skill and it can be improved. When people tell me they need more I time, I always say what they really need is more skill (training)! Here are a few tips to help you become a better time manager.

Get real about your time-management challenges. What is keeping you from making the most of your time? Do you need more training? Do you have trouble delegating? Do you get sucked in by distractions? Are you a procrastinator? Are you realistic about how long it takes to do things? Once you start to understand the root causes of your time management issues you can take the appropriate steps to correct them.

Don't just manage your time; manage your attention. Getting focused is tough in really busy environments, but it is key to getting things done. As tempting as it is, don't multitask. Research shows that it does not lead to more productivity. In fact, it leads to less, and to more mistakes.

Also, know when and where you do your best work. Schedule your day accordingly, and do your hardest work during your most productive window of time (and in your most productive location).

Manage your schedule. Don't overschedule. You get behind and problems pop up and you have no time to deal with them. This really leads to frustration, which is not productive. Be realistic about time allowances for yourself and others. Also, let others know your schedule so they know what you are working on. This will help eliminate interruptions. Knowing that others know what you're supposed to be doing also holds you accountable.

Create a dashboard. Leaders have a tendency to work "in" the business instead of "on" the business. It's easy to get bogged down in busy work. It may feel good in the moment to check things off the list, but it feels bad to look at the clock and see that you've spent all day on B and C items and made no progress on A items.

A good way to do this to keep a dashboard in front of you at all times. This will help keep your organization's big goals top of mind. These are your high-leverage activities. Carve out some time each day to work on each of these things and delegate the rest. Remember the adage "Show me your calendar and I'll show you your priorities." If you don't schedule it, it's not really a priority even if you claim it is.

Take a few cues from Stephen Covey. I love Covey's book *The 7 Habits of Highly Effective People* and often recommend it. One of my favorite tips in the book is to do the most important things first. Sometimes we have really important things that have to happen that day, but we don't think they will take long and we put them off to the end of the day. Inevitably things go wrong (that we didn't anticipate) and we are out of time to really fix it (creating missed deadlines or project failures and a heck of a lot of stress). Do the most important things first, when time is on your side. It will change your life!

I also love Covey's tip about beginning with the end in mind. For every task or project, start with the completion date and work backward. Break the project up into chunks and set mini-deadlines. Too often people underestimate how long things will take and overestimate the ease of getting it completed. Starting with the end in mind makes it likely to build in enough time to get the project done.

Keep your to-do list updated. We've all heard "plan the work and work the plan." Your list is how you put this principle into practice. There is just no way to hold everything that needs to be done in your mind. I have found the most effective people I know work from a list. Updating this list every day (or at the very least every couple of days) keeps critical items from dropping off and helps you stay mindful of what the most important items are so you can focus on them first.

Also, know ahead of time what you're going to do first thing in the morning. This will help you kick your day off quickly and get things rolling. When you start out like this, momentum takes over, and you tend to keep working at a good pace for the rest of the day.

Frequently review the list with the boss. Teach direct reports to do the same. This is especially important in today's deeply complex workplace where things change quickly and we must frequently reassess and recalibrate. Yesterday's priority may not be today's priority. When time is limited (and it's always limited) we need to make sure we're always working on what really matters—and we don't know what we don't know. Keep your list in front of the boss.

Schedule time for deep work. If you don't, it won't get done. Actually write valuable time down on your calendar and stick to it. This may mean closing yourself up in your office and asking employees not to interrupt you for a few hours. For sure you will need to shut down your email and social media so that you can be fully present and focused. Without planning for this time to happen you won't be able to do the deep, uninterrupted thinking you need to get big chunks of work done.

Minimize digital distractions. Email, social media, and digital devices fracture our attention and focus. If you don't manage digital distractions they will manage you. For example, schedule time each day to check voice mail messages and open emails and stick to it. Do not have instant messaging appear on your devices. Whether on your computer, phone, or tablet, every time a message appears, the eyes and mind wander. You lose concentration and that means valuable minutes.

Do all you can to touch something only once. This is particularly true with emails. Yes, there are things that you will flag to respond to later. However, the more often you can handle something as soon as you open an email, the more time you create. Often the immediate reply saves lots of time instead of having to reopen and respond.

Limit the number of people you put on the "to" line of emails. The more people on the "to" line, the more people feel the need to respond and the more cooks in the kitchen. Be clear on who needs to respond and by when (and be clear that those included on the "cc" line do not need to respond.)

Don't let a few missing details stall a project. Keep it moving forward. You can always drop in missing information later. In general, it's more important to meet deadlines than to hold out for perfection. I always say that 90 percent is usually good enough.

Cut time from all meetings. We tend to get stuck in scheduling meetings for 30 or 60 minutes. Why? Drop 30 to 20 and reduce 60 to 40 for a start. You will find you will get right to the point and cover same amount of material. Still hold the other minutes in case you do need more time and it provides time for any follow-up needed.

Break the procrastination habit. This is a major time sucker. The more time you put between you and the project, the less you remember and you have to waste time reacclimating yourself with the details. It also narrows your choices, as a tight timeline often takes certain options off the table. Most of all, it can turn a fairly routine project into a stressful pressure cooker.

Keep your workspace clean and organized. Having to search through stacks of papers for the one you need wastes more time than you might think. Besides, visual clutter leads to mental clutter. You'll work more efficiently when you don't have a lot of stuff lying around to distract you.

Avoid idle chit chat. Relationship building is important so you do need to spend quality time with employees and coworkers. But make sure you're talking about things that matter and not wasting the workday. Plus, if you aren't careful, it can easily turn into a gossip session.

Problem prevention is key. Anticipate problems and head them off. Thinking things through up front allows you to foresee what might go wrong and put processes in place to prevent that from occurring. There are lots of other ways to anticipate problems: doing a "post mortem" after a less successful project, seeking input from employees (who may be more familiar with the logistics of a process and see problems that you can't), and making sure you communicate with transparency and clarity.

Be responsive, not reactive. When we're driven by a sense of urgency (maybe even panic) we tend to make knee-jerk decisions that can send people down the wrong road. When we're reactive we may often lash out emotionally, which can upset employees. This not only harms your working relationship but is also counterproductive. Stay calm. Think it through up front. Carefully consider the options and then make a decision.

Take a break! You aren't saving time by working through lunch. When you walk away from your desk for an hour (or at least half an hour) you'll be rested and ready to jump back in when you return.

Enlist help whenever possible. You don't have to go every project alone. Enlisting a few helping hands when it makes sense to do so will help keep you on track and will very likely make the project a more rewarding task. The best way to meet a deadline is often to get a team of people together to help. (Get the boss's permission first, of course!)

Now, we're moving into an area that deserves more explanation. See below to learn more about why leaders have trouble with delegation and how you can learn to do it well.

Some Thoughts on Delegation

It can be hard for some leaders to delegate. New leaders especially may have trouble moving from *doing* to *leading*. It's easy to see why. Leaders are often promoted because they're good at what they do. They get into a mind-set of "By working harder and longer I can be more productive." In other words, they see a direct connection between effort and outcomes. This is no longer true when they become leaders. No matter how much effort they put in, it may not be enough to achieve the results they want (unless they are very skilled at coaching others).

Yet, of course, no one person can do everything. You just need to change the way you think about delegating. It's a way of moving action to the best place in the organization. It's a way to better manage resources. Not only does it free you up to work on other, more crucial items, it creates a training ground for others to become more valuable. This is a platform for building respect and trust. It develops employees and creates more engagement in the organization.

Here are some tips to help you get better at delegating:

Really get to know employees. Effective delegation requires you know everyone's strengths and weaknesses. Giving someone a task that they can't do well frustrates and upsets everyone. On the other hand, matching their skill set with work from your "to-do" list can give them a real chance to shine.

Give really great instructions. We delegate when we are busy so we often don't take the time to do this up front. Yet by giving great instructions we make it less likely that the employee will have to redo the work. Instruct, then ask them to give you a written summary of what they heard. Share the project's deadline and ask them to prioritize accordingly.

Keep in mind that the employee will want to jump right in and start working. In tense situations, it's a natural instinct to do this. But without full working knowledge of the entire project, it's unlikely the employee can determine where their skills are most impactful. When you give good instructions you make it less likely the employee will make assumptions.

Know that it might take longer, *the first time*! Let them make a few mistakes. This is part of the learning process.

If they need resources or additional training, make sure they can get them. This is part of setting them up for success.

If you give them the responsibility, give them the authority. Don't make them have to keep coming back and asking permission for every detail. This wastes their time and yours. Also, let others know they are now in charge of this project so they will be more likely to cooperate.

Let them know it's better to check in if they have any questions. They might think you are too busy otherwise. In fact, it's best to schedule regular check-ins. Likewise, tell them if they see a better way to run it past you first. They may not know all the variables. (This falls into the "making assumptions" category we've already discussed.)

If it doesn't go well, have an honest conversation about why. Don't just pull the project with no explanation. Also, reassure them that all is not lost. Let them know that you will delegate something else to them in the future.

Thank them very publicly when the delegation is successful. This inspires their commitment as well as the commitment of others.

Finally, teach employees to delegate. Explain that is a way to manage resources, not a sign that they don't want to do the work. When they see you modeling this, they will be more likely to follow suit.

Keep practicing all of these time management behaviors. The better you get at them, the more you will be freed up to do other things. You get more effective.

It is amazing how much better you'll feel when you learn how to take control of your time. It forces you to think about what is most important to you and allows you to carefully distribute your most precious commodity (your time) to the tasks that matter. In the end you will feel a far greater sense of accomplishment, you'll be less stressed, and you'll be able to focus more on the people and activities outside work that you truly care about. It's no exaggeration to say that good time management skills can truly change your life.

9

Grace Under Fire:

How to Manage Yourself During Stressful, Busy Times

There's no question about it: today's workplace can be stressful. The long work hours, the endless flow of information, the competing demands on our attention, the rapid changes and uncertainty they bring—all of these factors and too many others to list can make us feel perpetually overwhelmed and out of control if not managed well.

Yet the conditions that lead to stress are not "bad." They're just reality. Every time in history has had its own set of stressors. And if you are a productive person your plate is *always* going to be full. When the conditions are managed well, they create incredibly fulfilling work. We can be grateful for that while also acknowledging that it's not easy. But I always like to come back to what Scott Peck said in *The Road Less Traveled*: "Once we truly know that life is difficult—once we truly understand and accept it—then life is no longer difficult."

It's the leader's job to deal with the conditions and problems that lead to stress in a way that keeps everyone on track. (Think about it this way: if things always went well we wouldn't even need leaders!) And middle managers face even more of a challenge because they have to balance the needs (and stress) of their team with the expectations (and stress) of their leaders.

All that said, how we manage ourselves in the middle of the storm is everything. Relationships are defined by how we behave under stress. Difficult, busy times can put strain on relationships, but they can also forge stronger bonds if handled the right way. It all comes down to your ability to show grace under fire. When your team sees you pull things together and navigate them out of a tricky situation, it can be a huge credibility builder. Conversely, when they see you fall apart, it can create a trust deficit that is hard to recover from, even when things settle down.

How you behave when times are bad truly defines you as a leader and sets the tone for how others manage the situation. If you create a culture where people fall to pieces when things get tough, it will be too stressful for employees (and they will likely leave), productivity will suffer, and all this ultimately will make your job harder.

A few suggestions for managing yourself with grace under stress:

First, eliminate as much stress as you can by being a well-run organization. Work to create a best odds environment for eliminating problems. Things will go wrong from time to time. You can't control everything. However, there are lots of things you *can* control. Make sure you have good processes and procedures in place for eliminating avoidable headaches. For example:

- Plan for disaster by learning from mistakes and fixing the culprits.
- Identify stress points and think critically about who they impact. What is causing increased workloads? Use this evaluation to decide where to delegate work, and identify team members who might need additional support. (Don't lower expectations. This will only breed excuses and erode performance over time.)
- Say no to some requests. This way you don't have to scurry around trying to do them and then later explain why you didn't get them done.

Learn to prioritize (and teach others to as well). A big to-do list should not freak you out. Everyone is busy and they should be. Just use the list to work in a sensible order (evaluating daily what is most important). Often we try to close out small tasks to make room for bigger ones, when what we should be doing is prioritizing our to-do list and staying focused on the things that really matter. Just "getting things done" may feel good in the moment but what really matters is getting the big things done.

Simplify when things get stressful. Bring order and clear thinking to chaotic situations.

Keep an eye on what really matters, and what can be cut away. A good leader can make a potentially crushing workload feel manageable. By taking a cool and methodical approach, you can make a huge difference in helping others stay focused and productive and keep their stress reactions in check.

Create a culture of calm. Be sensitive to the messages you're sending out. Model calmness when things are chaotic. You teach your employees how to behave based on how you behave. The things leaders do, both positive and negative, get mirrored. And research shows that the ripple effect of negative emotions is considerably more intense than that of positive emotions. If employees see you panicking, they are likely to panic. If they see you staying calm and focused on solutions, they will mimic this behavior as well.

Also, try not to show physical signs of stress. Wringing your hands and pacing around anxiously will not make things better. In fact, it will likely make your employees *more* worried and stressed out, negatively impacting their performance.

Don't blow things out of proportion. Do everything you can to keep a level head. Sometimes our tempers flare when things are stressful. Try to avoid letting little things turn into big problems. When leaders lose their cool, problems only escalate. People get upset and their productivity plummets. Plus, explosions can cause long-term damage and tank a leader's credibility. In the end, all of this means more time fixing avoidable problems.

Be careful about the words you use and the stories you tell. Avoid using words like "slammed" or "overwhelmed." There is nothing wrong with stating that you are busy, but how you talk about being busy and carry yourself impacts others. It has a ripple effect. Just because you are stressed doesn't mean everyone else has to be. Don't bring your stress to the people.

Keep the past in its place. Leaders can generate lot of stress for themselves and others by rehashing mistakes and misses. Yes, frame these mistakes as learning experiences but don't keep talking about them over and over and telling the story. It just becomes gossip at that point. Instead of focusing on past challenges, look for what's right and constantly celebrate bright spots. This shifts the focus inside the organization.

Don't pretend to be fearless. A common mistake leaders make is to pretend that everything is fine when it clearly isn't. Sometimes acknowledging that a situation or negative circumstance is real, and possibly even scary, is the best way to build trust with your team and get them to invest 110 percent on solving the problem. This is not the same thing as getting bent out of shape. You can be honest and calm at the same time.

Put some ground rules in place to help others manage stress. Busy, stressful times are when you need cooperation and engagement the most. Yet it's during these times that tension builds, emotions run hot, and people explode or otherwise behave badly. Recognize this and put a plan into place to help people deal with frustrations and conflict in a way that won't harm the team's ability to perform. For example, you might ask everyone to be mindful of their tone when communicating while under pressure. You might also ask others to jump in and help when they see a coworker getting overwhelmed. As a leader, you not only need to manage your own stress but also help others manage theirs as well.

Master a few tactics for calming yourself down and teach others to do the same. If you feel yourself starting to get overwhelmed by stress, here are a few ways you can calm yourself down quickly:

- Control your body. Don't let it control you.
- Walk away. Take a 20-minute break. Sometimes you have to do this.
- Go for a walk. Physical activity is a great stress reliever. It can help you calm your mind and get some much-needed clarity around what needs to happen next. Little breaks like this are a great opportunity to plug in your headphones and listen to a quick song or audio file that might help relax you. Even better if you can get outside, even for just a moment. Most of the time, a little natural sunlight can make a big difference in our mood.
- Open up your body and take a few deep breaths. Put your shoulders back, head up, and stand tall. Try to intentionally quiet your mind. This is a technique professional athletes have known and used for years to manage stress before a big game. Opening up the body allows for better blood flow, and deep breathing puts more oxygen in the blood and can help minimize the impact of cortisol (the stress hormone).
- Count backward from 10. Do it twice if you have to. Shifting your focus from the problem at hand to a relatively simple task can help you come back to your work with a fresh set of eyes. It

also helps your brain reset and refocus. Moving the focus away from your problem and onto an abstract thought, even one as simple as counting from 10, will also help you calm down, and control your emotional response. It forces you to use a different part of the brain.

Create a best odds plan for staying healthy. This gives you the stamina you need—both physical and mental—to cope with stress and keep going. Sleep well, eat well, stay hydrated, and generally take good care of your body so you'll be in tip-top shape mentally. This requires discipline and planning, but health and well-being are too important to leave to chance. Good habits fall to the wayside during busy times. You may be tempted to skip lunch because you're too busy to eat or you stayed up till 1 a.m. working. Remind yourself that this is counterproductive. You can't perform if you are sleep-deprived and sugar-crashing because you didn't take time to pack a nutritious lunch and ate from the vending machine instead. If you aren't healthy you won't be able to cope when stress levels kick into overdrive.

Be resilient/learn to reset. Setbacks will happen. Leaders must be able to bounce back quickly and continue to move forward even when things appear to be falling apart. Resiliency is essential as leaders need to have the mental wherewithal to offer support and continue to direct their teams. Being resilient comes from having good coping skills, supportive environments with a lot of psychological safety, a strong sense of optimism, grit, and having the mental and physical stamina to sustain and move through stressful situations. Work on all of these factors but also know that resiliency also comes with growth.

As with everything else, experience counts for a lot. The more seasoned leaders will be better at handling stress just because they have had so many years to learn to cope. They've seen what can happen when they don't handle stress well and they are more motivated to change. If you are a new leader, know that this is a skill you build just like everything else. Use the tools and tactics discussed earlier and know that it gets easier every day.

As Paul Harvey once said, "In times like these it is helpful to remember that there have always been times like these."

10 Change the Way You Think About Change

If *there are two things people hate, it's change, and the way things are.* I recently heard this quote and it really hit the nail on the head. There have been so many books written on change that the subject can feel overwhelming, but it certainly isn't going away. There will always be forces pushing for change and forces pushing back against it.

A few years ago, I read an article in the *Harvard Business Review* entitled "All Management Is Change Management." The author made the case that we live in a state of constant, rapid improvement and in this environment, change isn't anything "special." It is no longer a big deal, but instead, it should be part of your daily routine. The process of change is ongoing and ordinary. It has to become the essence of how we live.[1]

I like the idea of shifting our mind-set about change. Change isn't some remarkable disruptive event. It just *is*. It's a constant feature of our world. It's not going anywhere. So we need to respond by making sure a healthy attitude about change is woven into the fabric of our everyday lives.

A good analogy is the outdated notion of "going on a diet." We all know that we can't "go on" a diet because that implies that at a later date we'll "go off" the diet. If that happens we will never be able to sustain weight loss. Instead, it's much more sustainable to adopt a healthy lifestyle. No peaks and no valleys, just a constant striving toward healthy choices. The same is true of our approach to change. We have to commit to nonstop forward motion, every day, otherwise we fall behind.

So how do you make change part of your culture and part of the ongoing way you work? The key is to put formal processes in place to ensure it becomes part of the everyday routine. A few suggestions:

Change your language. Stop thinking (and talking) about change as some big, overwhelming event. Start thinking (and talking) "continuous improvement" or even "evolution." You're figuring out how to get better and better, and that's a good thing.

Make it one of your company's values to question all processes. Never stop looking for ways to make them better. And think small. There is always room to make small, incremental improvements. These really add up over time.

Hold people accountable for making ongoing improvements. Make sure all employees are responsible for identifying ways to make things better. They are on the ground and more intimately familiar with processes and will be able to notice things you won't. Give them good examples of what you are looking for. For example, you might help them recognize and act on growth opportunities. Improvements can also come from people learning new skills or finding new ways to show value to customers or expand a service offering. When they get really intentional about new ways of looking at customer needs, new ways of delivering customer service, or new ways of strengthening customer interactions, the ideas really begin to flow.

Develop a process for collecting ideas. How will the ideas be gathered and evaluated? Create a clear system for how "changes" will be implemented.

Keep an action log of ideas. Fill it with things that seem inefficient or that you'd like to improve. It's often easier to spot these in the heat of the moment or when things are going wrong. Jot them down as they happen. Look for reworks, time wasters, or frustrating processes. Those are often easy to revise and you get some quick wins.

Reward ideas. What gets rewarded gets repeated. Rewards don't always have to be monetary. Even if it's just a thank you note or public praise, people love feeling rewarded and recognized and will continue taking action to get that good feeling again. The positive reinforcement is training them to keep on thinking about improvements and innovations.

Celebrate small wins. Reward and recognize big successes. Maybe a measurable improvement occurs, or you sign on a big new account, or you get some praise from a happy customer. Anytime there's a chance to say thank you to a senior leader, a department, or the whole company, take it. Positive reinforcement is a powerful driver for change.

This is a win-win strategy. Once people have shifted their thinking about change, they'll start to see results. They'll get excited about their new track record of innovating and improving. And before you know it you will see that you've accomplished something every business owner seeks: employees who are highly engaged. They've become owners, not renters.

Implement these steps and you'll be well on your way to being a high-performing organization. But as mentioned earlier, there's another related topic that needs to be addressed: pushback. To a certain degree pushback is normal and natural. But there will sometimes be people who are adamantly opposed to change and you need a strategy for dealing with them.

Don't Let Change-Resistant People Block Progress

Most organizations, whether private, not for profit, or government, have people with many years of experience in their most senior positions. This experience has a benefit and a downside. The benefit lies in the senior leader's ability to handle situations, their track record of good performance, and the presence of skills that have been developed over time. The downside is that, due to past success, the leader may be reluctant and at times resistant to adapting to a different way of doing things. This resistance to change often leads to an organization that does not keep up with shifting employee and customer needs.

For many years I owned an outcomes firm specializing in process improvement. We were usually hired when the top person in the organization saw a need to get better, had tried doing it their way, were not seeing the results they wanted, and finally became willing to move into the uncomfortable world of change. Why? Because they believed that achieving results was more important than their comfort. These are the "walk the talk" leaders.

So when the top leader would bring us in, here is what usually happened: the top leader would explain that they were hiring us to move performance in certain areas. Most senior leaders who reported to the CEO knew of us, and a few were the ones who were not getting the results. The top leader would explain that this would mean some changes. For example, there would be more measurement of employee engagement, productivity, quality, and customer service. A new leader evaluation tool would now be used to evaluate performance and there would be more accountability. There would be a mandatory increase in leadership development. There would be more transparency. While there were more changes, these were the items that impacted the senior leadership the most.

As you might have guessed, some of the senior leaders were concerned about all the changes. At times they would even try to convince the top leader not to hire us. However, the middle managers and the hourly employees were happy about the changes. They liked the fact that they were going to be surveyed and asked for their input on everything from supervisor feedback to recognition to work environment.

The managers liked that they would have clear goals—which took the politics out of performance reviews—and would receive 64 hours of development. Being a manager is very hard. They were happy that we wanted to help them do their job better. Employees felt good for the same reasons. They liked being able to give input to decision makers. They liked being rounded on by their supervisor to see what is going well and what is needed to do their job. They particularly liked being involved in hiring their coworkers.

My experience is that change is hardest on the people at the top. It means changing methods they have used for years and habits that have become deeply engrained. It also means adjusting to the reality that, in many ways, they will get worse before they get better. Here are some tips for helping top leaders cope with change and dealing with pushback at all areas of the organization:

First, get comfortable with being uncomfortable. Creative tension is what Peter Senge, the author of *The Fifth Discipline*, describes as the space that exists between where people are now and where they want to go. I went to one of his conferences years ago, and he said people know where they are, they know where they need to go, and in between is discomfort. No one likes to be uncomfortable, but it is a necessary part of growth.

Like change itself, creative tension and pushback are normal. Get comfortable with them and help employees get comfortable as well. Leaders who know how to manage these aspects of change have a much greater chance of success.

Meet one-on-one with each direct report. Share where the company is going, the changes you plan to make, and that you're 100 percent committed to making them. Explain you need them to be 100 percent on board (and if needed share what this looks like). Ask what percent on board *they* are, and if less than 100, discuss what it will take to get them there. Share that if they cannot be 100 percent committed by a certain time, they must leave the organization. Usually most get on board. If this leads to an exit, it is likely good for all concerned.

Share with senior leaders that you realize change is hard. Tell them that you, like they, will be uncomfortable—however, you and they must role model the change for others. Just acknowledging this can make a big difference.

Take time to explain the *why* to them and the entire organization. Nothing is more powerful than knowing the reasons behind the change you're being asked to make. Whether it's to make life better for customers, to improve performance and profitability, or (and this is usually the case) both, understanding *why* keeps people motivated as they push through discomfort to learn new skills and override old habits. This is true not just for your senior leaders but for middle managers and all employees, so communicate the *why* over and over again.

Don't take pushback personally. Seek to provide clarity. Pushback may have nothing to do with the proposed task. It can very well be the person is trying to figure out how they will be affected. They could be pondering "what's in it for me?" They could be feeling anxiety or fear. Let's say I work for a company that is about to roll out a new piece of technology that is supposedly going to speed up our processes, increase productivity and profitability. Sounds great, right? But *before* I get too excited, I'm going to want to know:

- Is there a chance I could lose my job?
- Will this new technology reduce my hours?
- Will my job change?
- If it does change, will there be training?
- How much time will I get to adjust?
- What if I *can't* adjust?

It's best if you can answer all these questions right away or if not, let them know why right away. Transparency and clarity will go a long way toward acceptance.

Expect your best employees to push back. Why? They are high performers. So, change will mean they will regress a bit until they understand the new process. Meet with and share with them that you know change is difficult, things will get worse for a while, but you have confidence in them and you need them to role model how to handle the change.

Don't lower the bar. A leader's job is to make sure the tension is not so great the employees give up. There are two ways for the tension to be reduced: One is to lower the performance bar. You have heard complaints before, such as "There is too much on our plates." "We have too many priorities." "Everyone is unhappy." Of course, a leader could lower the bar to address complaints, but the company wouldn't last long after they did so. The second way is to motivate your employees to close the gap between where they are and where they need to be. More difficult than lowering the bar? Of course. But it always pays off in the end.

Don't declare victory too soon. I've seen many companies bring in outside consultants to help them improve performance. Due to the cost of these outside experts, an increased level of attention and accountability is brought to the table. The experts suggest tactics and initiatives, these organizations implement them, and either nail their desired results or come close to achieving them. This is when they declare victory. Eventually, over time, the intensity that led to the achievement fades away. The spotlight begins to shift to other areas. This is when slippage starts. If not checked, it can lead to a regression and a tumble back to the original starting point.

That's not even the worst part. The worst part comes later, when another initiative begins and employees know it won't last. It didn't before so why should it this time? And those people who don't want any change at all have had their resistance reinforced. They'll wait this one out, too, and tell their coworkers "I told you so" after quick gains are followed by a gradual slip.

Change is challenging but not impossible. Most times you *can* teach an old dog new tricks. Research shows the brain has an incredible ability to learn, master new skills, and make new connections even at an advanced age. I've seen many seasoned leaders change their behaviors and habits in positive ways and have seen big improvements made inside companies. Approach change the right way and you'll be amazed by the success that can happen.

Note

1. Robert H. Schaffer, "All Management Is Change Management," *Harvard Business Review*, October 26, 2017, https://hbr.org/2017/10/all-management-is-change-management.

11 Embracing Discomfort:

Why Allowing Yourself to Be Unsettled Makes You a Better Leader

> *People wish to be settled; only as far as they are unsettled is there any hope for them.*
>
> —*Ralph Waldo Emerson*

This quote sums up why it is so difficult being in any role that involves people and performance.

Over the years, as I have spoken to and interacted with many individuals and groups, I have recommended various actions that, if implemented, would improve performance and lead to better results. Quite often I get pushback. A common response I hear is, "I am not comfortable doing that." But the truth is, much of a leader's job is spent being uncomfortable and leading others through discomfort as well.

The challenge is that marketplaces shift. Customer needs evolve. New technology emerges. Employees come and go. All of these factors mean that what once worked for your business might not be working now—or at least not as well as it once did. There may be lots of room for improvement. All of this means there is going to be disruption. It's natural and inevitable. And it's far better for your company to disrupt itself than to let the marketplace force changes on you. If you wait and a competitor takes all the business, it will be too late! Being proactive, not reactive, will also let you strategize and better control the process.

A good example of self-disruption is finding ways to differentiate yourself from competitors. This can feel uncomfortable to people. For example, I often suggest letting customers or clients know your training and experience up front. Think of a scenario in which a chef comes out, introduces themselves, and reviews the dinner options. What if the chef added where they had gone to culinary school and also mentioned their other training and experience? This addition not only impresses the people hearing it but informs them in a way that they can share it with others. This creates effective word of mouth.

The pushback I sometimes receive is that saying these things sounds like "bragging." My response is, "No, it creates a feeling of confidence in the customer." Check the information on a poster advertising a concert, a play, or a performer. You'll see that well-known, positive things are shared: if the performer is a winner of a Tony Award on Broadway, or how many top-40 hits they have, or if they are a best-selling author or a Pulitzer Prize recipient. There is nothing wrong with letting people know you are well-qualified and good at doing your job.

Self-disruption may require getting people comfortable with new processes. For example, years ago, when I was a healthcare administrator, we discovered peer interviewing can help benefit retention. So the organization announced that a potential employee's coworkers would be part of the interview process and make the final decision on whether the candidate would be a good hire. Many leaders were reluctant to do this. One even quit. Yet after peer interviewing was implemented and it worked, the reluctant leaders jumped on board. The person who had left even asked to come back (which they did but in a nonsupervisory role).

Yes, taking actions that make us uncomfortable is hard. Taking actions that create discomfort in others is just as hard or even harder. Yet that is part of the leader's job. If we are to do our job right it's inescapable. Here are some tips for handling the "unsettling" that you will experience as a leader and cause others to experience.

Realize that discomfort is normal. As M. Scott Peck wrote in his book *The Road Less Traveled*, "Life is difficult . . . Once we truly know that life is difficult—once we truly understand and accept it—then life is no longer difficult."

It's best if disruption comes from you and the organization and not from outside sources. Make time to work *on* the business, not just *in* the business. Reevaluate your company regularly. Schedule a time to pick apart your processes and systems. Keep that date, no matter what. Take it one department at a time. You are likely to find what you think is happening inside your company—perhaps even the very basic fundamentals—isn't happening. This will give you a chance to step in and make needed change—to disrupt yourself.

Get in the habit of asking questions. Regularly ask employees what they think your biggest challenges are. What might the company do differently? What is holding us back? What is working well? (This may be the most important one of all and, in fact, you should lead with it.) Also, question customers on how you can better serve them, when and where you've exceeded expectations, and what problems you solve for them. Never be afraid to ask questions for fear you might not like the answers. If you don't ask, you won't know what you need to improve.

Own the messages that unsettle you and others. It is easy to blame someone else. Saying to the staff that you don't like it either, but it is the corporate position, impacts the company poorly. Let's say the yearly budget you are given is less than you had asked for. It will mean letting the staff know that more help will not be hired or a new piece of equipment will not be bought. As a leader you have a choice: you can deflect the pressure (and ease the discomfort you feel) by blaming corporate, or you can carry the message yourself. Those who carry the message themselves and take ownership of it are the real leaders. (See Chapter 23 for more on we/they.)

Don't be afraid to ask corporate to explain something further so you can better understand the decision and explain it to your staff. It will still be uncomfortable, but it is the way a good manager handles things. As Jim Collins wrote in the book *Good to Great*, great leaders own tough messages and take responsibility for less-than-desired results.

Understand and explain the *why*. To return to my first example regarding sharing with a customer or client your education, training, and experience, here is a story. I went to a dermatologist about a spot on my face. The physician looked it over, took a small sample, sent it to pathology, and asked me to wait for the results. About 30 minutes later, he told me it was skin cancer and needed to come out. I then (nicely) asked him where he went to medical school and did his residency. He answered that he graduated from Vanderbilt University School of Medicine and completed both his residency and a fellowship in dermatology there.

Was he bragging or self-promoting by telling me his background? No. He was reducing my anxiety and building my confidence as a patient. That's the *why*. Once people understand the why behind what they're being asked to do, they are almost always willing to push through the discomfort and adopt the behavior. As leaders it's our job to convey the why in a way that people can truly hear and understand.

Make it a cultural standard to immediately admit to mistakes. This is one of the most valuable things leaders *and* employees can do because owning up to mistakes allows you to quickly fix issues and course correct. Yet the prospect of admitting mistakes is deeply unsetting to people. As a leader, model this behavior. Say "I was wrong" when needed. And make sure it's psychologically "safe" for others to do so as well by not punishing mistakes. Make it clear that mistakes are a necessary part of learning and growth.

Urge employees to get in on the self-disruption, too. Once your employees see that you're constantly evaluating how the company is doing, they'll get involved, too. It won't be just you the business owner or leader who is looking for ways to improve. It will be everyone working together. Those closest to the process (employees) are often the best ones to disrupt and improve it.

The beauty of regular self-disruption is that it creates a culture inside your company in which people continually look for a better way to do things—a culture in which no one is satisfied with anything less than the best. Creating this kind of culture is worth the uncomfortable feeling of being a little unsettled.

Don't forget to recognize and celebrate what's going right. As you constantly seek to disrupt and unsettle yourself, you will also find that some things are going right inside your company. This allows you to celebrate the "wins" with employees and also to praise and reward your high performers. This keeps engagement and morale high and encourages employees to work even harder and smarter.

Remember, discomfort is neither good nor bad. It's a byproduct of change. It gets a bad rap at times, yet some change can be very good. That new baby, new job, new house, car, city, or even that new understanding—all of these are uncomfortable, because all mean an adjustment in some manner. Yet most people will ultimately agree that once the dust settles, the change was worth the temporary discomfort.

Leadership means unsettling ourselves and others. The most effective leaders realize that being unsettled is part of the process of life, and they work to understand and role model this truth.

12

Clarity Counts:

How and Why Leaders Should Give Clear Guidance on Rules

As I mentioned earlier, I recently had the honor of sharing a stage with Admiral Harry Harris, the US ambassador to South Korea. It was interesting to hear what he had to say, especially when comparing the similarities and differences between public and private leadership.

Admiral Harris's military background was apparent when he talked about how important it is to give clear guidance. He said, "People follow orders better than they read minds."

This really stood out to me. Imagine how catastrophic it is in a military situation when people aren't absolutely sure what they're expected to do. And I've also seen disasters unfold in the business world when clear direction wasn't given.

This notion of clear guidance is also highlighted in a new book called *Go Long: Why Long-Term Thinking Is Your Best Short-Term Strategy*. It's a really short book—just 100 pages—and is a series of case studies that give a history of times when important decisions created huge turnarounds for companies.

There's one story in the book about Alan Mulally, who was CEO first at Boeing and then later at Ford Motor Company, where he is credited with the company's $48 billion turnaround. It talks about how he kept a handful of rules on a single card and repeated them over and over. He used this same card for 45 years!

This clarity made it easy for employees to follow the rules and for managers to hold them accountable. In fact, *Go Long* points out that Mulally rarely had to fire anyone. His clarity around the rules, and his insistence on holding employees to them, caused people who couldn't change to realize it and to leave voluntarily.

Clarity enables engagement and drives execution. People like clear boundaries. Vagueness and uncertainty (or mind reading, as Admiral Harris said) create anxiety and stress and make mistakes far more likely to happen. Most people truly want to do good work, and they like leaders who make that easy for them.

Clarity also promotes accountability, fosters teamwork, improves morale, and cuts down on workplace drama. For all of these reasons, clarity accelerates results and boosts the overall performance of your company.

Many times we think we're being clear when we're not. What we think we said and what others actually heard can be shockingly different. Great leaders realize this truth. That's why they make sure that people are 100 percent clear on the rules. Then, they reinforce those rules at every opportunity. They live by them and make sure others do, too.

A big part of creating clarity inside your company comes down to those structural building blocks we discuss later in the book. Companies with a lot of structure in place—by which I mean foundational pieces like mission, vision, and value statements, official written standards of behavior, a system for setting and communicating clearly defined goals, an objective evaluation system that measures performance on those goals, and so forth—tend to be good at creating clarity.

But even if you haven't yet put all the building blocks in place (or if you're still working on them) you can take a cue from what worked for Alan Mulally and Ford. A few tips for making their approach work inside your company:

Spend time really thinking about the rules and values that matter most to you. Boil them down until you have a short list—maybe five or so—of guidelines. (Use simple wording. Nothing fancy.)

Give a lot of specificity. Don't just tell them what to do, tell them how to do it and put some hard timelines in place. In the book *Switch*, Chip and Dan Heath tell the story of how Don Berwick, CEO of IHI (Institute for Healthcare Improvement) was frustrated by the number of deadly medical errors. He announced a prevention initiative, declaring that in 18 months, he wanted to save

100,000 lives. (His actual language was June 14, 2006, at 9 a.m.) To achieve this, he proposed six specific interventions hospitals should undertake and made it easy for them to participate. By the deadline, 122,300 lives had been saved. The Heath brothers credit his clarity and specificity for surpassing the goal. Their expression that "Some is not a number and soon is not a time," is one that really reminds us to get clear on expectations.

Share them with the entire company. Post them on the website and your break room wall. Send them out in emails and texts. Maybe even write them on a card like Alan Mulally.

Any time an employee doesn't understand a rule, repeat it. Don't worry that you've already said it. People will be grateful for the clarity.

Always **hold yourself accountable to the rules.** Integrity is crucial for leaders. Nothing will make the rules more clear than when leaders model the behavior.

Hold others accountable, too. Because you've made it clear what the rules are, you can assume that when people don't live up to them, it's an issue of "skill" or "will." If it's a skill issue, provide the necessary training. If it's a will issue, then as tough as it is, you have to let the person go. (Nothing drives high performers away as quickly as low performers who go undealt with.)

Take advantage of teachable moments. Use mistakes or mishaps as a way to hone clarity. It can be a real learning opportunity and a way for leaders to clarify things that might not be crystal clear. Use the opportunity to narrate which rule or value might have been compromised. It may even spotlight the need for a new guideline.

A commitment to clarity is at the heart of every high-performing business. When everyone knows the rules, respects them, and relentlessly follows them, you can achieve amazing things. Also, learn to recognize when clarity is a problem and fix it right away. In *Switch*, the Heath brothers say that what looks like resistance or pushback might just be a lack of clarity. If people don't know exactly what you mean, it will be hard for them to get things right.

13

Face Conflict Head-on:

Why Conflict Resolution Is the Ultimate Business Skill

No one loves conflict and confrontation. We all want to be liked and accepted, and very few of us enjoy hurting people's feelings.

Unfortunately, as leaders, we *must* be able to handle conflict or we're not doing our job. We need to be able to hold tough and productive conversations with others, and address conflicts that arise inside the organization.

As business gets more and more complex, ever-more-difficult situations arise. In some cases it can feel like all leaders do all day long is solve problems. If we don't get on top of them right away, small issues will turn into big issues. They will snowball until they poison every corner of our culture.

At a time when unemployment is at record lows, competition is fierce, and consumers have endless choices, a strong, healthy culture is a must. You want to attract the very best people and work with the best vendors. This depends on your ability to create and maintain healthy, productive relationships—and conflict resolution is a cornerstone of that skill.

Here are just a few examples of how problems inside a company expand when leaders perpetually avoid conflict:

- Unresolved conflicts lead to communication breakdowns. This harms teamwork and collaboration, and, before you know it, productivity and innovation begin to suffer.

- Big, important decisions are delayed or not made at all. Unfortunately, with most decisions, someone will be unhappy. But when you put off "pulling the trigger" too long, you can miss out on great opportunities for your business.
- High performers leave. Conflict-avoidant leaders often won't confront employees who aren't pulling their weight, nor will they give needed promotions that might upset someone else. Resentment around the unfairness grows, and your best people get fed up and leave.
- In extreme circumstances, conflict avoidance can result in legal action. For example, if you don't sit down and talk to an unhappy vendor over, say, a payment dispute, they may end up suing. If the leader is simply willing to sit down and have an open and honest conversation early on, such issues can usually be avoided.
- When you habitually avoid conflict, people *will* notice. They'll come to see you as a weak leader. When that happens, others will begin to go around you, leave you out of important initiatives, or just steamroll over you.

Clearly, conflict avoidance is bad for your company and your career. The good news is that there are things you can do to improve in this area. For instance:

Hold up the mirror. What might be causing your conflict avoidance? . . . Maybe you grew up in an environment where issues were swept under the rug and you never learned how to disagree with others. Or maybe the opposite is true: there was constant conflict in your family and so you shy away from it now. Understanding why you dislike conflict is the first step in making a change.

. . . And how does it manifest in your behavior? Do you go along with others even when you know they're wrong? Do you hide in your office or miss meetings you should be attending? Do you "lay down the law" and then leave the room so that you don't have to deal with those who might disagree with you. (Believe it or not, conflict avoiders can also be bullies!) Once you zero-in on your own avoidance patterns, you can take steps to change them.

Keep your larger sense of purpose top of mind. When you remind yourself of the *why*—why you're in business and why you chose the career you chose—you'll be more willing to bite the bullet and fix what needs fixing. You'll know that if you don't, you're ultimately hurting the cause you care deeply about. Then, your values won't let you *not* address the issue.

In fact, it may help if you don't think of it as conflict at all, but as resolution. You're getting a problem solved and that's a good thing.

Be really clear about what you expect from others. Conflicts often arise because people don't know what you expect from them. They go down the wrong path or make mistakes because you gave vague direction (or none at all), and then you're forced to confront them. Most people want to do the right thing and will if they know what the right thing is. So make sure they do, and you'll head off a lot of conflict on the front end.

Rely on strong systems and processes, along with objective metrics to take bias and opinion out of the equation. I've always been a fan of focusing on outcomes. This goes along with my previous point on clarity. For example, when employees know up front what you expect—and there are objective metrics in place to determine whether they met the goal or not—conversations become about results, not perceptions. Things are less likely to get personal and heated.

Don't put off hard conversations. They won't get any easier. When you must have an unpleasant conversation with someone, do it right away. The longer you wait to address a problem, the more it escalates, and the worse the fallout becomes. What might have been a mildly uncomfortable encounter can become a shouting match.

Focus on solutions rather than finger pointing. When you must hold a tough conversation, or find resolution with someone you expect to disagree with, approach them from a "What can we do to solve this issue?" standpoint. By reframing a tense encounter as "constructive conflict," you're less likely to come across as judging, blaming, or shaming. This simple shift keeps things civil.

If you're wrong, say you're sorry. Sometimes you really do "own" the conflict you're trying to avoid, or at least a big portion of it. Take responsibility. People will respect this, and you'll go a long way toward defusing their anger.

Get some coaching or conflict resolution training. There really is an art to settling disputes and conflicts. In many ways, the ability to have tough conversations in a timely manner is the ultimate business skill. If you don't have that skill, you owe it to your company, your employees, and yourself to master it.

Make resolution a part of your brand. Be known as the person who never sweeps things under the rug. People will come to expect this from you and this will shape their behavior. For example, they will realize that if you don't address something it's probably because you're not aware of it. They will start bringing issues to your attention.

All of this becomes easier when you realize that conflict really isn't a bad thing. It's how work gets done, progress gets made, relationships get stronger, and people grow professionally. You will never love conflict, but you can learn to live with it and get better and better at navigating it. In the process, you'll become a better and better leader.

14 Reaching Resolution:

How to Have Tough Conversations Without Damaging Relationships

In the last chapter we talked about why it's so crucial for leaders to be able to handle conflict and have tough conversations. We also touched on the "how" from a 10,000-foot-view perspective. Now I want to get more granular. How, exactly, do we have difficult conversations with employees, partners, vendors, and others in the workplace?

The goal with tough conversations is twofold. One, you want to solve a problem. Two, you want to do it without damaging your relationship with the other person.

An organization is simply a network of strong, collaborative, mutually beneficial adult relationships. The better the relationships, the better the company. The good news is that tough conversations can actually strengthen relationships and help both parties grow personally and professionally *if you handle them the right way.*

Before you go into a tough conversation, ask yourself these three questions:

1. *Am I being fair and consistent?* It's important that you don't have one set of rules for one person and a different set for another.
2. *Am I too focused on being "right"?* Just because you may disagree with someone doesn't mean they are wrong. People have different experiences and points of view. Life isn't always about "right" or

"wrong." When you have that attitude, you probably won't even listen to what the other person is saying.

3. *Do I need to call in a witness, document the conversation, or consider other legalities?* Depending on the nature of the situation, you might. If you're not sure, consult an HR rep or employment attorney.

Now, here are some tips for having difficult conversations:

Stay focused on preserving the relationship. It *is* possible to convey difficult messages while still treating the person with dignity, respect, and empathy. This conversation is just one moment in time. If you damage the relationship, you shut down future opportunities for collaboration and innovation. Keeping this in mind should help you stay civil, focused, and sensitive to how you say what needs saying. In fact, tell the person up front that the relationship is important to you.

Consider that you might be wrong. Go in with an open mind. You're diagnosing, not condemning. You may not know all the variables causing the person to do the things they're doing. Often, we hear something totally unexpected that shifts our perspective. We can always be wrong! Knowing this and being willing to admit it is the sign that you're a strong leader. It will also help you be a better listener.

Before you call the meeting, get clear on what you want to say. Be sure you can express up front what the problem is, how it's impacting others, and what must change. Stick to these points and don't go off topic. Be prepared with hard metrics if you can: "You missed the sales goals by 37 percent last quarter" or "You've been absent 13 days in the past 6 months." Productive conversations are grounded in facts, not observations.

Schedule a time to discuss the issue and give the person a fair warning beforehand. Otherwise, it gets blurted out in the moment and results in unfavorable outcomes. For example, say, "Chris, I'd like to chat with you about what happened with the Jones account earlier this week. Can we meet tomorrow morning at 8:00?" This gives the person a chance to gather their thoughts and prepare emotionally for the meeting. Ambushing people or not being transparent about the nature of the discussion creates anxiety and breaks down trust.

Meet on neutral ground. It's usually best not to call the person into your office. This shifts the balance of power to your side and puts the other person on the defensive. It's better to meet in a conference room or a restaurant. This sends the signal that this is a solutions-centered discussion, not a dressing down from an authority figure.

Seek to be collaborative, not authoritarian. You want the other person to work with you to make things better. Outcomes are so much better when the person feels a sense of ownership for the solution. Ask positive questions, "How are you feeling about our partnership? What factors do you think led to this issue? Do you have any ideas on what both of us might do differently moving forward?" Don't exhibit a "my way or the highway" attitude. It's good to listen to the other person's perspective and to compromise when you can. It shows the person you respect and value them. Might doesn't always mean right and the loudest voice shouldn't always win.

When you ask questions, give the person time to gather their thoughts. Don't just talk to assert your point of view or fill up silence. This comes across as you steamrolling over the other person. This is especially important when you're dealing with an introvert who needs time to think before they speak.

Listen actively. It's all too easy to spend your time calculating your response and not really listening. Try to stay focused on understanding what the person is saying, both verbally and nonverbally. Summarize what they are saying, and confirm that what you think they said is actually what they meant. Trying to understand where someone is coming from is a way showing empathy. It helps them accept what you have to say, even if it isn't what they wanted to hear. When people don't feel heard or listened to, it's upsetting. It damages relationships.

Keep things civil. *Never* yell, insult, threaten, or bully the person. This should go without saying, but we're all human and emotions can get out of control. If things start to escalate, end the meeting and reschedule when you're both calmer. A single episode of bad behavior can tear down a relationship that took years to build. The person may appear to comply in the future but there will be an underlying resentment that affects performance and outcomes. The issue will get lost and the focus will be on your bad behavior. It's okay to take a break or come back later if you need to calm down. Remember, odds are good you'll still be working together.

End with an action item. Ideally, you and the person will both have a task to do going forward. This way you can schedule a follow-up conversation to see if things have changed for the better.

Most people will never enjoy tough conversations, but you can learn to get more comfortable with them. People often find they are the catalyst for growth. They get people unstuck and moving in a positive direction. When you think of tough conversations this way, you may feel more inspired to get better and better at having them.

15 Drill Down on Generalizations

"Everyone is upset."
"All the employees are feeling left out."
"Everyone is overwhelmed."
"People are angry!"
"I can't tell you who said it, but I thought you would like to know."

We all hear generalizations at one time or another. They can send us into a panic and cause us to act before carefully thinking things through. And one of the hardest lessons to learn in leadership is to be cautious before responding to them. I've never regretted pausing before taking action but I sure have regretted *not* pausing first.

When a leader responds without thinking things through they can create an even bigger issue, generating more worry and putting more energy into a situation than necessary. You may hear a complaint followed by "Everyone feels this way." But who is *everyone*? And why hasn't "everyone" come to the supervisor to voice their own concerns, instead of sending a single person to carry the message?

If you hear a generalization and just assume the majority of employees agree with it, you might make a knee-jerk change. Your reaction to the "crisis" that's not real might create actual problems in the long run. Afterward, you might discover that only one or two people actually wanted the change. Now the majority really *is* upset. Plus, you have reinforced that it's okay *not* to carry your own messages, which is the opposite of how things should work in an open, transparent organization. ("Owners" speak up and advocate for themselves.)

In my experience, it merely takes a few questions from a supervisor to make a sweeping generalization become smaller or disappear completely. As for the person carrying this message to the leader, though they may not realize it, they are actually hurting the person whose message they are carrying and they're hurting the organization as a whole.

When I was president of an organization, a vice president came to me and said "all the employees are upset." Bear in mind she was speaking for a division made up of 500 employees.

Fortunately, I knew to not rush to figure out what to do for all of these 500 "upset" employees. (I had already learned this the hard way at a previous job.) So I slowed down and asked a few questions. "How many employees have you spoken with?" I asked. The number dropped quickly. She had been in one department that morning and it was in a group of fewer than six.

I followed up with another question: "What are they upset about?" She said "They have staffing concerns." By asking what the concerns were, I learned that the organization didn't have permanent staffing issues, but one specific issue with staffing that morning.

With just two questions, "all the employees" had gone from being a large group of upset people to being a very small group, and the problem we were facing went from being permanent to temporary.

It's not that we shouldn't continue to look into employees' concerns. We should. It is very important for a leader to be open to suggestions and constructive criticism. However, we don't need to react without a thorough diagnosis.

When a generalization occurs, don't just ignore it; investigate. Ultimately, by asking questions seeking specifics such as "How many?," "When?," "Where?," and "What?," the issues usually gain clarity and the solution is usually not as complex or difficult as it may have seemed at first.

Drilling down on generalizations can also be effective with your customers. I have found that when a customer has a complaint, getting the specifics helps you know how to respond, as well as put the customer at ease.

When I worked in healthcare, sadly, at times we let a patient and their family down. A family member would come to hospital administration and ask to speak to the person in charge. As president, that meant me. They might say that the whole experience had been terrible.

I would take the first step and apologize that we were not meeting their expectations. I would take notes. I would make sure we had a game plan moving forward. After that, I would see if they were willing to answer some questions. I would ask about their registration process. I would get their opinion on the hospital's security. I'd inquire about housekeeping, about physicians, about food. What about all of the nursing shifts? The lab? How about imaging?

Very often the person would start saying that many of those aspects were good. They would say, "I really liked them." When the person left, we still had some fixing to do. However, we had progressed from "everything" being terrible to a place where we knew exactly what had gone wrong. It also helps the customer to realize that perhaps, though we may not have lived up to expectations on one aspect of the experience, there were other aspects that proved worthy of their business and trust.

So the next time you hear a generalization from your employees, listen. But before you react and attack an ambiguous problem or take one person's word who's trying speaking for dozens, dig deeper. Most times, you'll discover the best way to take action.

Some things to remember:

People who deliver these generalizations are often the ones upset, but they may not have the confidence to express it as solely their concern. Ask yourself if this could be the case.

These messages are often steeped in emotion, which instantly makes them appear very serious. People are often angry at this point when they come to you. Remember that as you are listening to them and take a calm and designated approach. Don't match their energy; deescalate.

While it may be exaggerated in scope and severity, sometimes the problem is real. Take time to investigate whether there is problem that needs fixing.

Listen for key words like *everything, everybody, all, terrible, disaster*, and so forth. Words like these could be your cue that a generalization is coming! Train yourself to manage them appropriately by asking a series of questions to get to the bottom of things.

Ask people to carry their own messages. If someone is upset, encourage them to come see you and not send a proxy. It just allows everyone to get to a solution faster and helps build your relationship with employees. Discourage all anonymous reporting.

Get to the bottom of the situation, but don't overreact. Take a measured, decisive approach. Model calm behavior and defuse things as quickly as possible. Don't let a few disgruntled employees upset the whole group.

Do regular surveys. Measure what's going well and pinpoint what you need to give some attention to. Getting in front of problems goes a long way toward helping you avoiding these kinds of incidents.

Reward and recognize employees who do come forward with legitimate concerns. This will make others more comfortable speaking up and encourage them to carry their own message.

Urge people to solve their own issues when possible. Ask that when they bring a problem they also bring a solution. Even if their solution isn't workable and you still have to get involved you've sent a strong message about the importance of ownership.

Teach and encourage others to make "I" statements. This gets people in the habit of speaking only for themselves.

As leaders we frequently find ourselves fielding complaints and being asked to solve problems. We need to hone our "radar" so we can find the balance between overreacting and underreacting. It's not always easy but the more we practice taking a measured and judicious approach to the generalizations we hear, the better we'll become at focusing on the things that truly matter and teaching others to do the same.

II Optimizing Employee Performance

In this section we explore what exceptional leaders do (and don't do) to create a positive, productive, engaging workplace culture. Great leaders create environments in which people put forth their best efforts, grow, thrive, and find a powerful sense of meaning. They lead teams in a way that create results far greater than the sum of the individual efforts.

16 Creating a Positive Workplace Culture

How often does an employee come up to you and volunteer a positive statement? For example:

"It is a great day! Everyone who was supposed to work today came in."
"The systems are all working as they should be."
"I have the tools and equipment I need to do my job well."
"It is wonderful to work for a boss who is so appreciative of my work."
"Wow! These customers are so grateful for the service we are giving."
"Thank you for providing just the perfect amount of communication."

Probably never! Most leaders tell me they never hear those things. Employees don't hear a lot of positive messages, either.

Yet we need positive workplace cultures. No workplace is perfect (and sometimes negativity is called for), but an environment that's mostly positive makes people happy and engaged rather than cynical. Happy, engaged employees are more productive and creative. Positivity also improves trust levels in the organization, which leads to stronger workplace relationships and paves the way for better communication and collaboration.

Plus, when workplaces are positive, people enjoy coming to work. They feel a strong sense of meaning and purpose. Turnover is lower and the best talent is attracted to your company. Over time, all of this will lead to a higher-performing organization.

The challenge is that positivity doesn't come naturally to people. My experience is that negativity grows like a weed in a workplace, but a positive culture needs to be cultivated. Our natural tendency as human beings is to focus on what's wrong. This is a survival skill leftover from caveman days. Leaders in particular are problem-solvers. We believe our job is to zero in on challenges and solve them. We just aren't as good at noticing positives and bringing attention to them. Yet in a thriving workplace, we need to be doing this regularly.

We may assume that what's right is obvious and typically goes unspoken. But this is just not true. I have never had anyone approach me during seminars and say "the temperature is just right." Occasionally I do have people come up to me and say, "It's freezing in here" or "I'm burning up." During a break in the seminar I ask the attendees, "How many of you are too hot? Too cold? Just right?" Most of the time the "just right" wins by a large margin. But until the question is asked, the "what is wrong" seems to surface the fastest (and the loudest).

All this means is that as leaders we have to be deliberate and proactive about creating a positive culture. We can't ignore the negative, of course. But we can make an effort to grow the positive so that it outweighs the negative. Here are a few suggestions:

First, fix any big glaring issues that might be causing negativity.
Being a well-run organization takes care of a lot of negativity and frustration. When things are not working well (including relationships, processes, or equipment), it's hard for people to stay positive.

It's important to make sure employees have the tools they need to do their job and that equipment is in good repair. Poorly maintained equipment requires work-arounds, creating frustration and wasted time and makes employees feel like you don't care.

Also, are there any processes or leader behaviors that need to change. For example, are leaders as transparent as they should be? Could they be doing other things that are causing a breakdown of trust? Do employees have a voice and input into big decisions?

All of this will require some digging into the specific issues that may be causing negativity to thrive. Regularly ask if there are things that need to be repaired. Create a plan and assign someone to oversee the changes and let employees know you are working on things. Negativity often doesn't come from the problems themselves, but more from employees feeling leaders don't care or aren't listening.

Fixing the problems you already know about has to be the first step. Without tackling big cultural, process, and equipment problems, none of your efforts to spread positivity will matter. It has to be authentic.

Learn to lead from a place of "what's right." Learn to focus on the wins, bright spots, and what is going well. (This kind of positivity, just like negativity, is contagious.) Look for positives and accentuate them when you can. When we start with the positive we feel good about ourselves and the company. We feel our work is meaningful. This gives us the energy and feeling of ownership we need to take action. Coming from a place of positivity makes us *want* to make things even better. When we do this regularly our positive attitude spreads to others in the organization.

Measure employee engagement—and act on the diagnosis. This is another great way to uncover problems and frustrations (as well as what's going right)! It's important to diagnose the problem before you start treatment. Plus, regularly measuring engagement shows people you care. You care that they're treated fairly, that they feel psychologically "safe," that they're comfortable making suggestions, etc. Use a well-regarded and proven assessment tool to learn where any issues lie. Be transparent about the results and commit to solving the problems you discover.

Force low-performing employees to improve—and if they won't, ask them to leave. Dealing with low performers is obviously connected to the well-being of your company, but it's also a deeply important part of keeping the team happy. No one wants to work with those who don't pull their weight. Other employees have to pick up their slack and it breeds resentment and low morale. Allowing them to stick around could even prompt your best people to leave. If leaders don't deal with performance issues, other employees may think you aren't paying attention to who is actually doing the work.

This is why it's so vital to have a system in place for holding regular performance conversations with all of your employees—and the more often, the better. Everyone needs to be consistently coached toward improvement, but *especially* low performers. If you can't move them up you'll need to move them out. They are just too damaging to those who are making positive contributions and doing their best work.

Celebrate wins and bright spots every chance you get. A big part of creating a positive culture means communicating the great things that happen. When you hit a goal or land a big account or get a great compliment on one of your departments, talk it up. Put it in your company newsletter and on the bulletin board. Announce it at staff meetings. The more you share the great things that are happening in your company the more aware of them your people will become.

When something "big" happens, you might even want to take employees out to lunch or bring in a cake or doughnuts. Mini-celebrations go a long way toward creating positive energy.

While these things might seem simple and insignificant, they matter to employees. We've all gotten so busy that we have let some of these things fall by the wayside, but they make a difference. Take the time to reinstate small celebrations. The cumulative effect of these things can be significant. What gets rewarded and recognized gets repeated. (For more information on reward and recognition, see Chapter 18.)

Get in the habit of asking employees what's going well and if there are things they feel could be made better. My experience is most of the time the answers are positive. If not, leaders will have items to address. However, you still get a win because the employee feels heard and has input. This is a very important part of creating an environment of trust in your company.

If the person does not have a response, cultivate it. Ask questions like: *Did everyone come in today? Are the systems working? Do you have the needed supplies, product, tools to do your job today?* Again, chances are most of their responses will be positive. By starting with the positive you help people see the good in their workplace that often goes unrecognized.

Find best practices and move them throughout the organization. This is key to creating an environment where people can do their best possible work. If you discover that one department is doing well in a certain area—for example, if their communication is particularly good—find out exactly what they are doing right. Then teach people in other departments to do the same. In this way, you're making their jobs easier and everyone's results improve over time.

Enlist employees in the campaign against negativity and cynicism. Of course, there are no "band-aids" to turning around a negative culture. You really do need to identify and address big issues that might be creating cynicism. However, a certain amount of negative talk might just be habit. Tell employees that you want to make positivity one of your company's values. Spell out what positivity looks like in action and include it in your standards of behavior. For example: "I will not badmouth customers" or "I will not say anything about a coworker that I wouldn't say to their face" or "I will say thank you when someone helps me."

Regularly connect employees back to meaning and purpose. Sometimes people can lose sight of why they do the work they do. When this happens it's easy for them to get focused on the wrong things. This is when negativity and cynicism begin to thrive. You can help by reminding people about the difference they make in the lives of customers and coworkers. See Chapter 19 for some suggestions.

It's not always easy for leaders to shift to this way of thinking. For many of us, who may be dedicated problem-solvers from way back, it goes against the grain. Yet once you start intentionally focusing on the positive, and seeing the results, it gets easier. Positivity just feels good. Soon you will find yourself seeing more and more positives to celebrate and share—which creates even more positives to celebrate and share.

17

The Secret to Strong Relationships:

Manage the Emotional Bank Account

Leaders are only human. We work hard to keep our employees engaged, happy, and productive—and indeed, this is a huge part of our job—but there *will* be times when we let them down. Sometimes this is our fault. We snap at an employee because we're in a bad mood, or we make a mistake that makes their job more difficult. Other times, something happens that's beyond our control and we have to bring them bad news that upsets them or stresses them out. There are also times when we need them to go above and beyond the call of duty.

Hopefully, these bad times are few and far between—but they will still happen. And if you don't have a great track record of creating positive feelings in your employees, these infractions *will* have an impact on how they feel about you. If they don't feel good about you, it will be much harder to lead and influence them.

For all these reasons it's important for leaders to understand how the *emotional bank account* works. This is my term for the goodwill (or lack thereof) that we maintain over time with the people around us. Ideally, we should strive to keep our emotional bank account full. We do this by making frequent *deposits* of positivity. That way, whenever we must make a *withdrawal*, our balance is still high.

Building a positive emotional bank account means doing all you can to keep your relationships (with employees, yes, but also with fellow leaders, customers, vendors, and other colleagues) strong, healthy, and productive. When you do this consistently across the organization, morale remains high and your positive culture remains strong. A bad day or even a bad week won't derail things because you'll have the emotional capital in place to outweigh the negative feelings.

Get to Know Employees Through Rounding

To build strong relationships with employees, leaders have to build personal relationships and get to know them. It's almost impossible to make meaningful contributions to their emotional bank account otherwise. Employees are individuals, with their own likes, dislikes, personal preferences, and interests. We need to know a person's *what*—meaning the one thing that really matters to them, motivates them, and drives them forward. And we can't know this until we put in the time and make the effort needed to do so.

Of course, very few leaders have lots of extra time to burn! If we don't get intentional about making a real connection with our people it won't happen. That's why I've always been a fan of leader rounding. This means that a leader puts a system in place to ensure that they regularly make a one-on-one connection with each direct report. They schedule it and make it a priority, because if they don't, it won't happen.

Rounding is not a casual, off-the-cuff, "how's it going" conversation. It's much more structured and deliberate than that. At least a couple times a month (if not more frequently), meet with each employee and ask a set of questions aimed at getting to know people and making sure they have what they need to do their best work.

I advise leaders to start by making a personal connection. For example, ask "How's your family?" or "Where are you going on vacation this summer?" or "I guess your son is a senior now. Has he settled on a college yet?" or "Are you still doing community theater?" The idea is to make a personal connection with the person about their life outside work. This shows the employee you care about them as a human being.

Then, move to asking about their work life. I like to start with something positive, like "What's going well?" or "Who has been really helpful to you lately?" Not only is this a good way to identify people who need to be rewarded and recognized, I find it sets the tone for the entire interaction. The employee will be more likely to be helpful and cooperative when they are coming from a place of gratitude. Plus, they're left with a far more positive impression of you and of the company and their coworkers. Over time, this also trains them to notice what's going right.

Finally, ask questions to help identify ways you can help people do a better job. Are there roadblocks that are keeping them from doing their best work? Do they need more training? Are there any general improvements that could be made inside the organization? Is there anything you, specifically, can do to make their life easier or more rewarding? How might you be a better leader? Think of this segment of the rounding as an ongoing preventative measure—a way to reduce your chances of unintentionally making a withdrawal from the emotional bank account!

This is important: if the employee gives you feedback about something that needs to change, you absolutely need to act on it and follow up with them later. If you've taken action, loop back around and let the person know. If you can't for some reason, let them know why. Ignoring the employee's concerns is the worst thing you can do for your relationship.

In general, rounding is the best way to truly get to know your employees on a deeper level and figure out what their *what* is. Knowing what people really care about and following through with actions to help them achieve it is the strongest relationship builder I've ever found, but asking them then doing nothing will tank credibility.

We covered some of the relationship builders in the positive workplace culture chapter, but here are a few additional tips that will help you build a positive emotional bank account with employees:

Tell the truth, always. Be transparent and honest all the time. This is the only way to build trust as a leader, and it always pays off, even if you have to deliver criticism or bad news. People appreciate clarity and openness; it relieves anxiety and sets employees up for success. If employees ever have a reason to feel that you're being evasive or deceitful in any way, trust will be broken, and the emotional bank account will take a massive hit.

Ask employees for help with problems. People feel validated when they are asked for their opinions. They appreciate that you value what they think and are eager to help you solve problems when they arise. You might ask, "Jim, you've got a great sales record. Do you have any advice for our pitching strategy with this potential client? How can we get a home run?" This not only brings forth great solutions, but it gives the employee the win! Even if you could do it yourself, bring them into the fold. Not only will they feel good, it will develop their skills for when you really need to rely on them, and you will feel less anxious about handing off projects if they have a track record.

Say "I'm sorry" when you need to, and mean it. As a leader, your mistakes—aka withdrawals from the emotional bank account—can make people unhappy or complicate their jobs. When a mistake has been made—whether you lost your patience and snapped at someone, missed a deadline, failed to communicate vital information, or otherwise mishandled a project—own up to it immediately and apologize. Let the person know that you realize the negative effect you've had on them. Great leaders are able to say they are sorry.

Make things right again. Sometimes just saying "I'm sorry" isn't enough. A good apology includes three components: expressing remorse, acknowledging the harm caused by your mistake, and making amends. The last part might mean making a sincere gesture to set things right again. For example, you might give employees an extra day off to make up for the extra work they had to do or even send them a small gift like a flower arrangement or a gift card to a local restaurant. And be sure to let them know you won't let it happen again in the future.

Reward and recognize people regularly. Positive recognition goes a long way toward making employees feel good about leaders and about the job itself. Say thank you sincerely, publicly, and often. Write thank-you notes. Praise and gratitude are powerful builders of your emotional bank account with employees. (Much more on this in the next chapter.)

Great relationships are everything in business, but they don't "just happen." We must deliberately and proactively *make* them happen. Get intentional about building positive and productive relationships with your employees and you'll be amazed by how quickly you'll start to see results. Positivity is contagious.

Most people want to do their best work and they want to feel good about their leaders, their customers, and each other. As a leader one of your jobs is to help them bring those good intentions to fruition. By building up the emotional bank account, you're creating and sharing the currency that everyone will use to create a stronger organization.

18 Positive Recognition Changes Everything:

The Art of Rewarding, Recognizing, and Saying Thank You

The deepest principle in human nature is the craving to be appreciated.

—*William James*

Positive recognition is a powerful tool for creating a positive workplace and shaping your culture. Singling out and thanking an employee for a specific behavior goes a long way. The employee feels good about the action being recognized. Because recognized behavior gets repeated, the employee will continue to do it. Other employees see what actions are being positively recognized and often follow suit. Do this over and over, with all employees, and your culture will shift. What gets rewarded and recognized gets repeated.

Research shows that if you hear **three** "positives" to **one** "negative" from an individual, you feel positive about that person. If you hear two positive comments to one negative, it creates a neutral feeling. And if you hear one positive for every one negative—a ratio people have long thought to be sufficient to create a positive culture—it actually creates a negative feeling.

During speaking engagements, I often ask the audience this question: "If you receive a message from your boss and it says 'call me when you can,' is your first thought . . . *Oh, boy! Here comes more positive recognition*?" Usually they laugh. But when you think about it, this is not really funny.

Then, I ask another question: "When I asked your direct reports the same thing, what would their reaction be?" With wide-open eyes, the group quickly realizes their own staff would also be more likely to think *What have I done wrong now*?

I still struggle with the 3:1 ratio myself. So do most leaders. Why is this so hard?

One big reason is that we are hardwired to spot problems. We can spot what is wrong and fix it. When we move into leadership, we continue to solve problems and identify issues. These are valuable skills to have; however, it is quite easy to fall into the trap of not being very assertive in noticing what is right. That works against achieving results.

Another reason that recognition can be tough ties back to a question most of us have asked or heard: "Do you mean we should recognize people for doing their job?" Yes, we should. Organizations can get too hung up on only recognizing people for what they call "above and beyond."

Early on, should we be recognizing the basics like smiling at customers? Absolutely. But as the employee matures, so do the actions that get recognized. We recognize our children for doing some basics: from crawling to walking to getting potty-trained. As these tasks are learned, then the recognition moves to a higher level. Same goes in the workplace.

Stepping up your compliments, if handled correctly, can transform the performance of your workforce, improve morale, and make your organization a better place to work. It can dramatically shift your culture.

One big reason to say nice things about employees is to improve retention. Have you ever noticed that when someone resigns they are suddenly treated better than they have ever been before? They are asked, "What can we do to keep you?" Not only is the pay increase or new job title the person had previously requested suddenly offered—too late—they hear all sorts of nice things about themselves at their going away party. Why can't we say all of these things to employees *before* they decide to leave?

Of course, there will be times when a company just can't offer a pay adjustment, but it may not really be the money an employee is seeking. Often people really want appreciation and acknowledgment of their hard work and their good results. Reward and recognition for a job well done is free. We can *always* offer it and we should when it is deserved. In the spirit of improving in this skill, here are some guidelines that may help you as you move forward:

Let employees know you're committed to being a better leader. Even positive change can create fear and anxiety. If a supervisor has been light on positive feedback, then suddenly starts complimenting people, the first thought might be "What new medication is he on?" Explain to staff that you are committed to being a better leader and an area you know you need to do better on is positive feedback. You might tell them you did not want them to be concerned with the change when you suddenly start saying thank you!

Don't lose sight of the 3-to-1 ratio. Remember, it takes **three** positives to **one** negative for an employee to feel good about the messenger. Keep this ratio in mind as you begin your positive recognition campaign.

Be specific and be authentic. Saying "nice job" just pales compared to "Shannon, I saw how you took time to explain our product to that customer. This really makes a difference." And make sure compliments are legitimate. Otherwise, you will soon dilute the value of giving them.

Compliment in public. Customers like to hear employees get complimented. Coworkers notice what gets complimented and will move to the behavior getting positively recognized.

Don't think general compliments get the job done. Sure, there are times when a thank you to the entire work force makes sense. After the Cubs won the 2016 World Series, the management thanked everyone in the organization. But typically it's best to target compliments to individuals. Wide-ranging compliments can demotivate your strong performers if they see that poorer performers get equal recognition.

Regularly ask employees, "Who do you suggest I can recognize?" After you receive the name or names, ask why. For example: Jonathan says Mike would be a good employee to recognize. I ask why. Jonathan shares that during a very busy Blue Wahoos game, the concession lines were backed up and Mike jumped in to help even though this is not his normal stadium job. I approach Mike, share with him that Jonathan mentioned him, and praise him with specifics.

This accomplishes a lot. Mike appreciates Jonathan, which builds teamwork. Mike's willingness to jump in to help outside his role is reinforced. And they both feel good about me.

When you see an employee taking the right action, say thank you right then and there. It can be as quick as "Jimmy, when the person ordered their drink I saw how you greeted them, repeated the order, told them how long the latte would take, and when you gave it to them, you thanked them. That is excellent and makes for great service, which builds customers. Thank you."

Remember, small gestures of gratitude and celebration can make a big impact. Send out a company-wide memo congratulating everyone on winning that new account. Treat the company to doughnuts on a Friday. Send out birthday cards along with a small gift card for staff birthdays. We sometimes think we're "too busy" to do these things and we may think people don't notice or care—but they do. These are the kinds of quick wins that make people feel great and give them an emotional boost they'll remember in the future.

Tailor your "thank yous" to specific areas you want them to grow. For example, if you have one employee who tends to be a bit self-absorbed, you might consider only praising them for their work with a group. Not only are you recognizing them, but you are promoting collaboration.

Hardwiring a Thank-You Note System

Now I'd like address one of my favorite methods of rewarding and recognizing employees: thank-you notes. I've written many thank-you notes over the years, and it's something I still do today. Many are written to people in my home city of Pensacola. Often during the week I'll have someone come up to me, thank me, and tell me they have kept the note. Sometimes I'll walk into a business and the owner will show where they have put my thank-you note on display.

The positive effect of thank-you notes became evident to me as a 16-year-old at my grandfather's wake in 1967. My grandfather, L.L. Studer, had written countless notes. He congratulated people on new jobs. On awards. On accomplishments. These notes were written to people young and old—for becoming an Eagle Scout, for being named president of a service club, for promotions.

At his wake, the line of people waiting to talk to my grandmother Belle Studer was enormous. Many of them let her know the impact that one note from my grandfather had made on them. The next day, I found about four file cabinets with four drawers each. In them were hundreds of carbon copies of notes my grandfather had sent.

The dots connected for me. Though many of these people didn't know Grandpa, the fact that he took the time to write a note meant so much. This had an impact that still lives with me today.

I studied a number of tactics meant to create organizational excellence years ago, and thank-you notes came up in the top six. However, when looking more deeply, I saw that the impact was connected to more than just sending a note. How was it composed? How was it sent? Who was it from? All of these factors mattered.

Most of us have good intentions but we don't always follow up with action. That's why we need to put a system in place to make sure notes get written correctly and regularly. A few tips:

Handwrite the notes. I'm asked this a lot—"Should they be handwritten or is email okay?" While an email or text is better than no note at all, a handwritten note is much more impactful. A typed note is a close second in terms of effectiveness.

Be specific. A general thank-you note is better than no note; however, the magic is in the specifics. Spell out what the person did right and the positive effect it had on a customer, coworker, or someone else. (This is where you connect the employee back to the sense of meaning and purpose that keeps them giving their best effort.) Include some background information if appropriate. The more specific the note, the more impact it has.

Send the note to the home if possible. A note to the home of an employee leaves an indelible mark. It becomes a family conversation. I could write a book on stories I have heard over the years from people about the impact of a note received at home. It gives the employee a chance to share the work success with their family and creates a lot of good will. I was speaking to a large group and I asked the audience if they have ever received a thank-you note from their boss. Some hands went up. I asked one of the people how they felt. "Would you like to see it?" he replied. In the front pocket of his folder he carried the note he had received from the president of the company.

Create a system and have the notes come from the direct supervisor's boss, or better yet the person in the top leadership position. Since my days in Chicago in the mid-1990s I have set up a system in which each week selected leaders are asked to send me an email with the name of an employee, a customer, or a vendor. They also outline why this person should get a thank you. I then write a thank you to the employee, always letting them know I had gotten a note from their supervisor and outline what the note said. Then it goes to the employee's home.

This has so many great effects. It makes supervisors much more aware of the good work the staff is doing. It helps top leaders learn more specifically the great work taking place, some of which are actions and ideas we can scale throughout the organization. Finally, it makes top leaders more visible to the employees they may not see regularly.

When I outline the above approach I ask the organization I'm working with this question: "If you get a note from your supervisor's boss or the top leader in the organization that says they are writing due to the note they received from your direct supervisor, how does that make you feel about your supervisor?" The answer is always "Great!"

I then ask, "How does it make you feel about the person you received the note from?" The answer is "even better." Thank-you notes create a win/win/win.

Verbal compliments and written thank-you notes are extremely powerful methods of reward and recognition. There may be times, however, when it makes sense to go beyond words and give a small reward to an employee. This could be a gift card, a magazine subscription, or a celebratory meal. Just don't give cash as a reward—it doesn't offer the emotional and memorable experience that more tangible rewards bring.

I started out this chapter talking about the business impacts of reward and recognition. They are very real. Yet rewarding and recognizing isn't just a business thing. It's a human thing. Don't underestimate the impact you can have on others by letting them know they are appreciated and that their hard work has been noticed. Life can be tough. We can all use some positive feedback from time to time—it reminds us that our work has meaning and that we do make a difference.

19 Meaning, Purpose, and Engagement:

How Great Leaders Effectively Connect All Three

People crave meaningful work and a sense of purpose. We all have a deep need to know we make a difference in the lives of others. In fact, many times meaning and purpose are more important to people than making a lot of money. This is truer today than it's ever been. A recent Cone Communications study found that 75 percent of Millennials say they'd take a cut in pay to go to work for a values-driven company.[1]

It's no secret that employees who feel a strong sense of meaning and purpose do better work. They're more creative, productive, and loyal because they really care. That's why helping employees connect to purpose and meaning solves the number one problem on a leader's dashboard: engagement. *Nothing engages us quite like a sense of purpose. It also helps us engage others.*

Companies that figure out how to consistently connect the people who work for them to that all-important sense of meaning and purpose—creating engagement in the process—have a distinct competitive advantage. The effort from an engaged employee can take a business from average to great. It's not hard to see why.

The engaged employee is emotionally committed to working on organizational goals. They care about the work product. They understand the impact they have on the company's success. They take care of equipment and supplies as if they were their own. They understand customer satisfaction means more than just a happy customer. All of this leads to better word of mouth, more customers, and better job security and wages.

Top talent is drawn to organizations that provide meaningful work and places where they feel they can make a difference. If we want to attract and keep the best and brightest employees, we have to inspire in them a strong sense of meaning and purpose. We have to make sure they're deeply engaged in their work. In a tight job market like the one we're in right now, we can't afford *not* to.

It's worth noting that this leadership approach works for all generations. According to Gallup: "Understanding a company's purpose helps employees answer *yes* to the question 'Do I belong here?'" Gallup's research shows that ensuring employees have opportunities to do what they do best every day and emphasizing mission and purpose are the two strongest factors for retaining Millennials, Generation Xers, and Baby Boomers.[2]

This all begins with making sure you're the right kind of leader—the kind employees want and need to lead them. And it turns out that this type of leader has some very specific skills and traits.

What Kind of Leaders Drive a Sense of Purpose, Meaning, and Engagement?

Remember, most people don't leave their job, they leave their boss. The best leaders know this, and they strive to become the kind of boss that truly makes a positive difference in their employees' lives. They connect to employees in a "heart and mind" way, reaching them on both the rational, data-driven level *and* the emotional, passion- and values-fueled level.

An article in the *Harvard Business Review* points out that there are certain leader traits that make jobs more meaningful for employees:

- They are skilled at hiring for values and culture.
- They are curious and inquisitive.
- They are challenging and relentless.
- They are able to trust people.[3]

Here are a few of my own thoughts and observations on these traits and their connection to creating a meaningful work environment:

On values and culture-based hiring ... For employees to feel that their work is meaningful they need to fit in with the rest of the team. Collaboration connects you to others. Not only does this feel good, it allows people to solve the big complex problems companies often face. (It's unlikely a single person can do this alone.) If the values and culture are a poor fit for an employee, they won't work as well on teams. It's crucial to know how to hire people who will enhance the culture and make the company stronger.

To do this, look beyond the resume. The resume only tells one part of the story and doesn't reveal much about how they will collaborate with your team. There are two other big components that reveal more about the personality, habits, and the value system of the applicant. One is *behavioral-based interviewing*, which gives you a more in-depth look into how an applicant has handled situations in the past related to teamwork, customer service, problem solving, time management, communication, and motivation/values. The other is *peer interviewing*, which essentially means engaging coworkers who will work closely with the new hire in the interview process. Peer interviewing makes it more likely that the right candidate will be hired, and it also helps existing employees feel invested in that person's success.

On curiosity ... Curious leaders are interested in people and finding new ways to do things. They believe their employees know more—usually far more—about their area of expertise than they (the leaders) do. So they ask lots of questions. They want to know how their employees think, how they would make the company better, how they envision the future. They encourage and empower employees to dig deeper, to look at different angles, and to become good problem solvers. It creates an environment of constant learning, which is good for the company and fulfilling for the employee. Curious leaders also build stronger relationships.

On relentless challenging ... Great leaders never stop pushing employees to improve. They hold the bar high and expect others to do the same. This type of leader usually prefers an objective, metrics-based style of performance management. They are crystal clear on what success looks like and they link pay to performance. That means employees either meet their goals (which are tied to the organization's overall goals and mission), or they don't. There is very little gray area.

High performers thrive in this environment. They prefer clarity to vagueness. They like knowing what's expected of them. This is a fair system and most people appreciate fairness. Plus, when employees know how they will be evaluated, they will rise to the occasion. They'll self-engage. They'll find creative ways to meet their goals, then they'll feel a sense of accomplishment. They'll clearly see that their hard work contributes to the company's success. All of this feels good and creates a sense of meaning and purpose that drives them to do even better next time.

Also, great leaders don't just preach relentless self-improvement. They live it. And because they also tend to do a lot of mentoring and coaching, employees are inspired by their example.

On the ability to trust ... Leaders have to trust their employees to do the job they've been hired to do. And yet, it can be challenging for many to delegate and let go. The problem is that when employees are consistently "overmanaged," they stop thinking for themselves. They'll never find their wings and fly on their own. Instead of solving their own problems they'll constantly be looking for you to lead them out of the wilderness.

This lack of trust rarely serves the organization well. After all, when leaders constantly have to be in the thick of projects that employees are (or should be) perfectly capable of handling, they never get their own work done. In an increasingly complex world, there just isn't time for hand-holding. And employees won't feel the sense of purpose that comes from contributing in a real and meaningful way.

Some leaders naturally do these things well. Others need to work at them. The good news is that when you have the will to improve as a leader, you'll eventually find the skill.

How to Be a "Best Odds" Boss for Engaging Employees

In addition to these four big, overarching behaviors what are the other traits that create the best odds environment for promoting engagement and connecting to purpose? Here are a few leadership best practices that are especially effective:

The best leaders are very intentional about creating environments of engagement. It won't happen by itself. Organizations have to regularly and systemically work to perpetuate an engaged workforce.

They are approachable and open to feedback. The employee feels they can bring things to the boss and the boss is open and helpful in the conversation. The employee is not fearful of being yelled at or subjected to other forms of retribution. This makes for such a better place because these bosses find out about issues that may be hidden if the employee is scared.

They are willing to jump in and help employees. The boss is not shy about rolling up their sleeves and pitching in. When they see there is more work than the employee can handle, they don't go into their office, but get right to work. One of the best examples of this is after roundtable sessions when tables needed to be broken down and put away. The best bosses are the ones that jump right in and help. The same holds true in the workplace, whether it's a busy restaurant, construction site, or office.

They don't ask others to do anything they will not do. Great leaders don't pick and choose when to jump in. They are willing to do any task they ask others to do. So, when the locker room at Pensacola's Wahoos Stadium filled up one time with some rather nasty water, all the supervisors who were there pitched right in. This principle also relates to following the rules. I find that one of the most common leadership mistakes is holding employees to standards that you aren't willing to live up to yourself.

They get the basics right consistently. For example, the best leaders are predictable on fundamentals like providing feedback, holding people accountable for meeting goals, living up to agreed-upon standards, and making sure everyone has what they need to do a good job. They keep promises and admit when they are wrong. They are fair, transparent, and willing to freely share information. They value employee input. They regularly recognize and reward good performance. This consistency is key to creating trust and respect and creating an environment where employees can flourish. Knowing what the rules are and what to expect from leaders gives employees a solid framework for making decisions. It promotes independence, gets everyone aligned and on the same page.

They schedule regular training sessions with each employee to provide coaching and development. During these meetings, focus on a developmental goal you have for the employee or a goal the employee shares with you. The vast majority of workers—managers included—want to do a good job. Creating a safe environment to share developmental goals as well as providing coaching is paramount. It's important to prevent the (very common) situation where the only time a supervisor and employee meet is during an issue (usually a negative one). Actually, when things are going well is a great time to meet.

They show employees they care about them. They regularly ask about their families, their hobbies, and so forth. They acknowledge birthdays and other significant occasions. Make time to really talk to them, not just on a surface level. This is part of the "heart" connection in the "heart and mind" equation. Don't just go through the motions or pass the task off to anyone else. Really value it and take care of it personally.

They regularly connect employees to the mission of the organization. This is the "why" that allows them to feel a sense of purpose. People really need to feel they are making a difference. The "why" is what keeps them going when things get tough. Helping them "connect the dots" between their day-to-day job and its deeply meaningful outcomes touches their heart and fuels passion for their work.

It's this last skill that truly sews up the employee's sense of meaning and purpose and helps them get (and stay) engaged. This is not about manipulating or fabricating a sense of meaning and purpose. It's about consistently saying and doing things that allow people to engage with the meaning and purpose that's already there.

Notes

1. Alexandra Douwes, "Your Secret Weapon for Increasing Employee Engagement: Purpose," *Forbes*, May 17, 2018, https://www.forbes.com/sites/alexandradouwes/2018/05/17/your-secret-weapon-to-increasing-employee-engagement-purpose/#50166a9938ca.
2. Chris Groscurth, "Why Your Company Must Be Mission-Driven," Gallup, March 6, 2014, https://www.gallup.com/workplace/236537/why-company-mission-driven.aspx#2.
3. Lewis Garrad and Tomas Chamorro-Premuzic, "How to Make Work More Meaningful for Your Team," *Harvard Business Review*, August 9, 2017, https://hbr.org/2017/08/how-to-make-work-more-meaningful-for-your-team.

20 Help Employees Understand the Meaning of Their Work

Some jobs by their very nature *seem* more meaningful than others. But really, *all* jobs are potentially meaningful. All companies serve their customers, their stakeholders, and their workforce, and the employees are in a unique position to make a real difference. It's up to leaders to help people see this. Great leaders create an environment where employees feel valued (and valuable) and this is what connects them to purpose.

It's easy to assume that an employee understands the impact of their work. Through the years I have been fortunate enough to have substantial interaction with police, firefighters, TSA staff, emergency responders, teachers, researchers, healthcare providers, security officers, and social workers. When reading those job titles, wouldn't you think they *have* to know the great impact they make? They don't—at least not nearly as much as you think. In fact, research shows that 53 percent of workers wish they had more insight into the effect their contributions have on their company's success.[1]

The reality is, every job plays an important role or it would not exist. There is no such thing as a job that does not count. And yet, we tend to work in environments where an employee is more likely to hear about their work when there is a problem. It is assumed that the impact of work is obvious, and because of that, leaders are not taking time to emphasize to each worker the *why* of their job and the important contribution it makes.

Research suggests that while leaders may think they're doing a good job of helping employees understand their company's purpose, they really aren't. These statistics from a Deloitte survey show the disconnect:

- 47 percent of executives strongly agree that they can identify with their company's purpose, compared to just 30 percent of employees.

- 44 percent of executives say leaders set an example of living that company's purpose. Only 25 percent of employees agree.
- 41 percent of executives say the company's purpose plays a role in major business decisions, compared to 28 percent of employees.
- 38 percent of leaders say their organization's purpose is clearly communicated, compared to 31 percent of employees.[2]

Numbers like these make it clear: *It is the job of the leader to take time on a regular basis to help each employee understand the importance of their role and the impact it has on the organization.* While the contribution made by the worker may seem obvious, the leader needs to help them connect the dots.

For example, consider that person in the billing department, the one who may not see a customer's face day to day. They need to know that by doing a good job in accurate billing, it allows the organization to do better financially, which goes to pay employees. When they know this, it helps them more clearly see their sense of purpose.

Billing may not be thought of as "glamorous," but the reality is that human beings can find meaning and fulfillment in all kinds of jobs. We simply need to know we're working alongside others to make people's lives better. Interestingly, according to Forbes.com: "A study published by the American Psychological Association found that hospital janitors were amongst the most purposeful workers they surveyed."[3]

Here's a story I heard once that perfectly illustrates this point: when President John F. Kennedy was visiting a NASA facility, Cape Canaveral if I remember correctly, he asked each employee what their role was in the organization. As the president asked, one by one, each employee would explain what they did every day. President Kennedy then came across a man who did maintenance in the building. Kennedy asked him what his role was. "I'm putting a man on the moon," he said.

This response was an echo of the president's famous goal. More importantly, it showed how the maintenance worker connected the work he was doing to the overall mission of the organization. He understood his purpose and felt that he was doing important, meaningful work. He didn't see himself as an anonymous cog in a machine.

He wasn't just doing a "job" but working in alignment with others to achieve a mission.

Here are a few tips on helping your employees connect the dots on meaning and purpose:

Explain to each worker how what they do impacts customers and coworkers. Remember, making a difference doesn't have to mean saving the world. It can be as simple as being the best florist in town or being the restaurant that serves up the most delicious burgers and shakes. Narrate this to employees. Help them connect the dots on how they make a difference in people's lives and in the success of the organization.

For example, we work hard at the Pensacola Blue Wahoos to let the employees know the positive impact they have on attendees. From David the ticket taker saying "Welcome!" to Paula on the landing at the first flight of stairs yelling "Waaaahoooooo!" to Travis or Stewart saying hello at the second flight of stairs, to Treneshia the usher saying "Welcome, let me help you," every person contributes to making the fans happy. Great fan satisfaction means more people attend the games. More attendees mean more jobs. More jobs mean better quality of life.

Drill down on the *why*. An article in Inc.com (the one that shared the Deloitte statistics I referenced earlier) suggests going up to employees and asking them why they're doing the task they're doing. The author explains: "Their immediate answer might be because it's part of the project they're working on. Ask them why they're working on that project. When they give an answer, ask why again. Follow this chain long enough and you should eventually arrive at your company's mission statement."[4]

Connect with customers and share that you like to recognize staff. Ask if there any staff members they would like you to recognize and why. Being very specific about what they did or said (or both) to positively impact customers will mean more to the employee. It will also reinforce that behavior so the employee will be more likely to repeat it. Customer praise and gratitude can have a huge impact on an employee's sense of meaning and purpose.

Ask recognized employees who is helping them behind the scenes. Then, pass the message along to them. People who provide direct customer service will get the most compliments, so when recognizing these folks, ask them who supports them that the customer does not see. Think accountants, cooks and dishwashers, and other back-of-house employees. Take the time to recognize these people as well and connect them back to their role in the customer experience.

Share meaningful stories every chance you get. When you are talking to customers you will hear stories about how much your company's product or service means to them. Quite often, they will share details and expressions of gratitude that staff may not hear. Make it your business to make sure all employees hear those stories. Share them at staff meetings, in company newsletters, on your website and social media pages, and in casual conversations. Stories are very powerful because they resonate on a human level. People remember them. These don't have to be huge events. Simple things work just fine.

Finally, pay passion and purpose forward by thanking people outside your company. When you receive great service, whether it's from a TSA employee, a ticket taker at a theater, a server at a restaurant, or an usher at the baseball game, let them know they are making a difference. It's amazing how seldom they hear this.

Many years ago, my dear friend Norm Adams went up to a street cleaner in New Orleans to thank him for what he was doing and to share that his work made the visit so much better. Watching this, I could see the man's face brighten up. After Norm walked on, I stayed to ask the street sweeper a few questions. I asked how long he had been doing this work and he shared that he had been street sweeping many years. I then asked him how often people stop to say thank you. He told me this was the first time.

We can all help employees feel that powerful sense of meaning and purpose. Not only will our company's performance improve, everyone will enjoy their job so much more. There is nothing quite like going to work every day at a company filled with people who are fueled by a true passion for what they do. It makes every day a learning experience, an adventure, and a path for personal and professional growth.

Notes

1. Robert Half, "Seeking a Greater Connection: Majority of Workers Want More Insights on How They Help Their Company's Bottom Line," *The Robert Half Blog*, July 4, 2016, https://www.roberthalf.com/blog/management-tips/seeking-a-greater-connection?utm_campaign=Press_Release.
2. Adam Vaccaro, "How a Sense of Purpose Boosts Engagement," *Inc.*, April 18, 2014, https://www.inc.com/adam-vaccaro/purpose-employee-engagement.html.
3. Alexandra Douwes, "Your Secret Weapon for Increasing Employee Engagement: Purpose," *Forbes*, May 17, 2018, https://www.forbes.com/sites/alexandradouwes/2018/05/17/your-secret-weapon-to-increasing-employee-engagement-purpose/#318975b038ca.
4. Adam Vaccaro, "How a Sense of Purpose Boosts Engagement," *Inc.*, April 18, 2014, https://www.inc.com/adam-vaccaro/purpose-employee-engagement.html.

21 Psychological Safety:

Making It Comfortable for People to Tell the Truth and Take Risks

People sometimes share with me that their job is to make the boss *look* good. I usually reply that it's much more important for them to help the boss *be* good. Few things are more dangerous to the health of an organization than for leaders to surround themselves with people who only agree with them, or act like they do when in reality they don't. If the leader is clearly going down a wrong path, the people around them *must* be willing to speak up and push back.

This means people must feel safe enough to tell the truth. If not, you'll never be a high-performing organization.

Psychological safety is a subject that's been in the news quite a bit over the past few years. In fact, when Google conducted its internal research study Project Aristotle in 2015, it found that psychological safety was the most important characteristic in terms of what makes a team productive. In other words, effective teams are those in which people feel safe to take risks and speak out.[1]

According to Harvard Business School professor Amy Edmondson, who coined the term, "Psychological safety is a belief that one will not be punished or humiliated for speaking up with ideas, questions, concerns or mistakes."[2]

We may feel unsafe when a boss (or any coworker) yells, says hurtful or disrespectful things, threatens retribution, makes irrational demands, and so forth. The primitive part of the brain sees this behavior as life-threatening and the fight-or-flight response takes over. When this happens (or when we anticipate that it might happen) we can't think, much less speak up when something is wrong. And so we don't: we shut down and take the "safest" route.

There are many reasons we want employees to feel psychologically safe. Honest feedback is critical to the long-term health of the organization. Employees are closest to operations. If they don't share the truth about what's really happening, small problems could turn into major ones. They have day-to-day exposure to things the boss would never know. They will be less likely to be innovative if they are afraid to take risks and fail. They need to be comfortable making mistakes. We need to make sure they feel safe enough to speak up when there is a problem. And on a company-wide level our teams must be able to bounce ideas off each other, participate in strategic thinking, and strengthen action plans.

We live and work in an ideas economy. The only way for a company to get better and stay competitive is to cultivate a culture where employees regularly collaborate, communicate, and innovate. This is where new/good ideas come from. These are the so-called soft skills that are so vital and in demand right now. They simply can't thrive in an environment where people don't feel safe and free to share their ideas, perspectives, and feedback.

For all of these reasons, good leaders make it clear that we want and expect feedback, including critical feedback, and we need employees who are willing and able to give it. If not, we will never be able to improve as leaders, drive better performance, and bring out the best in employees. So how do we create a psychologically safe workplace? Here are a few suggestions:

Know the difference between *positive* feedback and *good* feedback. We all prefer positive feedback, but make sure you're not sending the message that this is the only kind you want from employees. Good feedback isn't always positive. It can be critical or even negative, but it's always thoughtful and honest. Reward and recognize this kind of feedback when you get it. And when you get positive feedback, ask that it be specific and supported by valid metrics of success and is not just a "pat on the back" from someone who is afraid to speak up.

Model vulnerability. Acknowledge your own mistakes and show that you learn from them. This goes a long way toward helping people see that it's okay to take risks and make mistakes.

Be aware of how you react to bad news. It gives employees clues as to how you will act when they bring negative feedback. Don't let them see you blow up when faced with a problem. When this happens, they feel unsafe and are far less likely to share what needs to be shared.

Don't shoot the messenger. Make it clear that it's always safe to bring you bad news. When you get upset with people for letting you know something is wrong, you squelch communication. People avoid telling you the truth while issues are still fixable, so they stay unresolved and continue to grow until one day they explode. Far better to make sure people feel completely comfortable telling you the truth, even when it's something you don't want to hear.

Don't play the blame game. Instead of focusing on who is at fault, focus on what to do now. Blaming solves nothing and it kills accountability. When they know they will be blamed, employees will go to great lengths to avoid telling you about problems that need to be fixed. Also, when people feel blamed they shut down and just do what you say rather than taking a thoughtful approach and helping solve the problem. Be sure not to demean or belittle when mistakes are made.

Intentionally create a culture where feedback is encouraged. It should be normal and expected that people give feedback to each other as well as to the boss. Explain to staff that you need to hear from them, especially direct reports, anytime they feel you are off track and/or there may be consequences you are missing. Ask questions like "What am I missing? What am I not thinking of?" Say "Please speak up; don't let us go down the wrong track." Narrate that employees are closest to the problems and see solutions that leaders may not be able to see.

Repeat and reinforce this message often. Make seeking out and giving feedback a normal part of the routine. Ask for feedback when you share an idea and give specific guidelines and time frames on where, when, and how. Put processes in place that get employees in the habit of asking for feedback from you and from coworkers at certain stages of a project. You want everyone to get in the feedback habit.

Demonstrate your openness to feedback by taking an opposite or flawed position or making a statement that's obviously untrue. If someone steps up and points out your error, tell them thank you. If no one steps up, explain what you did and ask what you can do to make the environment safer so that people will be more willing to speak up in the future.

Take their feedback seriously. When you get a good idea from an employee, use it if you possibly can. Even if something is not a good idea, explain why it may not work, don't just say "no." This teaches people that you really do want their input and you're not insistent on running the show yourself.

Create rules of engagement, and tailor them to the needs of the people in the group. The last thing you want is for someone on your team to get overly confrontational with (or in response to) feedback. When people feel attacked, it shuts down the flow of ideas. Put standards in place for how to manage giving and receiving feedback and for how to handle conflict. These guidelines should be responsive to the concerns of the group and the challenges they face. Break the golden rule: it's not about managing others how you would like to be managed, but figuring out how they need to be managed.

Nurture curiosity. Encourage people to ask why and question decisions. Even if they don't come away with a better idea or a way to improve it, understanding the thought process behind decisions will help them grow as thinkers and make them more likely to step forward when they *do* have something to say.

Practice active listening. Don't let people feel like they are shouting into a void. Pay attention to what they are saying and let your body language and responses reflect this. Paraphrase what you're hearing and repeat back to them. Respond to their ideas thoughtfully and respectfully. When you model active listening, employees are likely to pick up on this and do the same.

Embrace radical candor. Be direct. Don't be unnecessarily harsh, but make a point not to sugarcoat the things you say. Likewise, don't expect things to be sugarcoated for you. Most people respond well to transparency, clarity, and openness. People like knowing where they stand and what is expected of them. This style creates a healthy give and take between leaders and employees.

Get people together face to face as often as you can. Technology is a good thing in many ways, but it definitely has its shortcomings. For example, it can be hard to communicate tone with digital communication. Feedback is better given and received in a face-to-face interaction. Plus, it is just easier to build the trust and camaraderie that makes for great teamwork when all parties can see facial expressions and body language.

If someone is generally quiet or unresponsive, call on them to share feedback. Introverts in particular can have a hard time competing with louder voices in the room. They deserve to be heard, also. But also know that they may feel more comfortable expressing their thoughts in writing, after they've had a chance to process them.

Separate "truth sayers" from "troublemakers." Some folks are just going to always be negative or find a problem to vocalize. Don't let these people poison the well. Separate them and their feedback from the good feedback of others on the team. Rocking the boat is not always good, nor is it always bad. Just learn the difference between good feedback and disruptions.

Know the difference between a "skill" issue and a "will" issue and handle accordingly. Sometimes even when you've done everything you can to help people feel safe, an employee may consistently fail to engage or contribute on the level that you expect. Or maybe they constantly stir up trouble and make others feel unsafe. At some point you will need to determine whether this is a "will" or a "skill" issue.

If it's a *skill* problem, provide coaching or training. If they have a *will* problem you might need to have a tough conversation. Explain what the person needs to do to improve their performance, lay out the consequences if they don't, then follow up. Often you'll find the person *does* improve. If not, the best course of action may be to move them out of the organization.

Creating conditions that help people feel safe is one of the most important tasks of a leader. A leader's job is to help people do their best work as well as improve and grow so they can perform at an even higher level in the future. Psychological safety is the basis for all kinds of positive emotions like trust, confidence, and curiosity—all of which pave the way for vital skills like critical thinking, problem solving, and creativity.

When we help people develop and nurture these skills we give them a great gift. We set them up to thrive, not just inside our company but throughout their career.

Notes

1. Charles Duhigg, "What Google Learned from Its Quest to Build the Perfect Team," *New York Times Magazine*, February 25, 2016, https://www.nytimes.com/2016/02/28/magazine/what-google-learned-from-its-quest-to-build-the-perfect-team.html.
2. Keara Duggan, "How to Build Psychological Safety," *Medium*, September 13, 2018, https://medium.com/@kearaduggan/how-to-build-psychological-safety-35feed9e282e.

22

Know What the *What* Is for Others (and Communicate Your Own *What*)

What's your *what*? Knowing the answer to this question, and making sure others know it, is the key to creating great relationships. Everyone—whether they're a leader, coworker, employee, or customer—has their own "what." Learning what a person's *what* is takes time and effort but the results are worth it. This is true in all relationships, personal and professional, and the sooner you realize this the better off everyone will be.

First things first: what do we mean when we talk about the *what* in a workplace context? Basically, a person's *what* is what really matters to them; what motivates or drives them.

Take an employee, for example. When you know your employee's *what*, you have a much better chance of understanding their behavior and maximizing their performance. Every employee has one thing (or maybe a few things) that mean more to them than anything else. Knowing what these things are will help you know how to connect with and influence them. Acknowledging and paying attention to these preferences let them know you care.

Knowing each employee's *what* can also help companies retain their top talent. The *what* might be how, where, and when an employee prefers to work. It might be how they want to be recognized, what kind of training and development they want, how they like to communicate, how they want to receive feedback, what they are passionate about, and what it takes to get them engaged. It might be their desire to have leaders connect on a personal level by knowing a little about their families, what their favorite sport teams are, what hobbies they enjoy, and so forth.

Getting to know people on a personal level is essential for figuring out their *what*. For example, just recently a business in town hired a new salesperson. In getting to know him, his boss discovered he had a background as a graphic artist and really loved the work. The boss was able to get him involved in the graphics and this person started helping with designs that saved the business money and made the employee feel great. Knowing what makes a person tick is critical in all relationships.

Here are a few tips on figuring out your employees' *what* and leveraging it in a way that makes their life better and also benefits the company.

Take out the guesswork: just ask employees what they care about. Your employees will appreciate being listened to, and more often than not they will be happy to tell you what matters to them. It lets them know that you care, and also goes a long way in developing trust.

Here are a few key questions to ask an employee:
1. "What is something I can do as your supervisor to make sure this is a great place to work?"
2. "What are some areas you would like to be developed in?"
3. "What are some things you find demotivating?"
4. "Let me know what's going well for you."
5. "What energizes you?"

Pay attention to what they react to. Sometimes employees might not know how to articulate what their *what* is, or they might not be so forthright as to share it. Just pay attention and you can probably figure it out. What seems to excite them? What seems to frustrate them? Do their ears perk up when you start talking about a new and exciting project? Or do they seem more interested in hearing about the successful results of the project you just finished? What kind of situations and behaviors seem to get on their nerves? Noticing these patterns will help you identify their *what*, even if they might not realize it themselves.

Know that there may be more than one answer, and that it may change over time. People are often motivated by a variety of factors. Their most significant *whats* are likely to be pretty constant over time, but their secondary motivations may evolve based on things that are going on outside of the organization, as well as the pressures of their work environment. For example, if an employee is about to start a family, flexibility in their work schedule might start to be more important to them. They might prefer to travel less if possible. These desired changes may not always be doable but noticing them and making the effort to accommodate them really matter.

Write it down and share it with others. Most of the time you won't be able to deliver on a person's *what* on your own. You have to make it a team effort with others at every level of the organization. Once you are able to articulate a person's *what*, share it with everyone that they work with, and make it clear that it matters to you as well. This is especially important in your interactions with customers.

When I worked in healthcare, we used Physician Preference cards. It was simply a card letting everyone know how a physician wanted to get information, where and when to contact them, when they prefer to round, etc. This helped nurses and other care providers develop effective working relationships with physicians.

Likewise, knowing your customers' *what* will help you deliver on the things that matter most to them, and grow a relationship over time. Create a way to capture the customer's *what* so others can also know it. This helps keep a customer when there is turnover in the organization. All these things make the employees' life so much easier, too!

I found a great example of this at a barbershop that I frequent. They have many stylists, and customers rarely see the same one consistently. To make things easier on both the stylists and the customers, the shop created a system where stylists collect notes on how each individual customer likes their hair cut, with specifics and preferences. This lets other stylists know how to handle them, and relieves the customer's anxiety around seeing someone new every time. Plus, how many of us actually know how to describe how we want our hair cut?

If you can't honor a person's *what*, at least acknowledge it. We can't always do things in a way where everyone's *what* is considered. When that happens, acknowledge it and let the person know why it didn't work this time. They will at least know you're sensitive to it. This will go a long way toward keeping your relationship positive and harmonious.

Know your boss's *what*. When you know your boss's *what*, you have a much better chance of working with them in a way that they'll appreciate and value. Every boss has a few things that mean more to them than anything else.

Years ago, I had a boss who liked quick turnarounds. I couldn't just add his requests to the bottom of my to-do list. When I stopped assuming that I knew when he wanted it done and started asking him specifics about his timetable for needing the job completed, things got much better. On the rush jobs, it gave me the opportunity to discuss what items I could delay in order to meet his deadline. This approach got us aligned and helped us meet deadlines. I had another boss who hated complaining. I later figured out, it wasn't the complaining he hated, but he was frustrated that complaints were rarely paired with solutions. I learned quickly to bring a solution when I brought a problem.

Here are some key questions you can ask your boss to help learn his or her *what*:

1. "I want to be sure I'm meeting your expectations. What is the best way to communicate with you? How would you like to hear information? How would you like me to ask questions?
2. "What are the things that are the highest priorities in this role?"
3. "When you think of great employees and what they do, what comes to mind?"
4. "Is there anything that drives you crazy that I need to avoid?"

Make sure everyone knows your *what* as well. Now, take everything we've discussed in the previous tip and flip it around. When you are a leader, your direct reports want to know what your *what* is. They want to know how best to work with you. They appreciate it when you don't make them guess. Explicitly state, "Here's how I like to work." Be as specific as possible. In fact, it's best to write it down so there is no confusion and they don't forget. Most people crave clarity and directness because it helps them prioritize tasks, helps them deliver projects in a way that you'll appreciate, and eliminates the anxiety caused by vagueness.

Work relationships are often not that much different than other relationships. Get to know a person, pay attention to what matters to them, and honor it when you can. Acknowledge it when you can't. It's a winning formula that promotes trust and respect from all parties.

23 Don't Resort to We/Theyism; Don't Let Others Practice It, Either

I magine that you're holding a performance review with an employee who (like most employees) is hoping for a pay increase. Unfortunately, you also know it's not in the budget. Because you hate to disappoint this person—and because you don't want her to think *you* think she doesn't deserve more money—you say, "Well, Sarah, I fought for your pay increase but you know how they are over in Corporate. Sorry, they're saying it's not in the cards this year."

That's we/theyism. It happens when a person positions themselves in a positive light by making someone else the "bad guy." Many leaders resort to we/they regularly, not realizing how harmful it actually is. Typically, this is not a deliberate choice but a fallback position of leaders who haven't been trained not to do it. They say things like:

"If it were my decision the answer would be yes, but upper management says no."
"Human resources won't let you do anything around here."
"It's above my pay grade."

While we/they can make the leader seem like a hero by "fighting for" the employees, it has a deeply divisive effect on your culture. It can make employees feel adversarial toward leaders, and one department feel resentful of other departments—feelings that, in turn, cause communication breakdowns and hinder teamwork. Perhaps worst of all it fosters a victim mentality and discourages people from having an ownership mentality—after all, if the leader doesn't "own" company decisions, why should employees?

So, in the earlier example, what should the leader have said to Sarah instead of blaming Corporate? Perhaps it could have been something like "Sarah, you know it has been a rough couple of years. Sales are down 15 percent and no one is getting raises right now. But we have a great team, we're all working hard, and I'm confident we can turn things around. In fact, if you have any suggestions to improve results, we'd love to hear them!"

When we get in the habit of explaining the why and taking ownership, it promotes trust and transparency. By positioning things in a positive way, it creates a feeling of unity. This can dramatically improve morale and set the stage for better teamwork. Setting the right example will show employees there are better ways to approach challenges than finger pointing and blame shifting. As leaders, we can set the right example and discourage employees from resorting to we/theyism, too.

A few tips:

To detect we/theyism, look at the metrics. When you measure employee engagement, the data can reveal this kind of divisiveness. If there is a big gap between how employees feel about their direct supervisor versus top management, you may have a we/they culture. The first step toward solving a problem is admitting you have a problem.

Carefully watch your wording. The next time something goes wrong and you feel a we/they moment coming on, stop and think before you speak. Are you about to put someone else down or shift blame, even in a subtle way? If your impulse is to say something like "I just forwarded the info HR sent over" this could come across as blaming HR. Instead, change it to something like "I'm sorry this information was wrong! Let me research this. I will find the updated numbers and get them to you as soon as I can!" See the difference?

When someone uses we/they in your presence, counter it by defending the other party. Imagine that an employee rolls their eyes and says, "Well, of course Finance won't approve our marketing budget. They throw cold water on everything!" You might say, "Well, it's not easy to keep our company financially strong in a tough economic environment. I think they deserve a lot of credit for that. Anyway, I have found when we're able to defend our budget with good market research and solid projections, the CFO will sometimes reconsider. Let's take another look at our proposal and see how we can shore it up."

Look for opportunities to manage up others. This sends the signal that you do not participate in we/theyism. Managing up is simply making the effort to position others in a positive light. The scenario we just discussed is a good example of managing up the Finance department. But you don't need to wait until you hear someone being "managed down" to manage them up. Get proactive about it. Never let a chance go by to say good things about other leaders, departments, and employees. The more you manage up others, the more others will follow your lead.

Promote open, honest, transparent communication. This is about telling the truth and admitting when you make a mistake. It's about carrying your own messages and insisting that others do as well. It's about not being afraid to have tough conversations and telling hard truths. It's about making sure people feel psychologically "safe" enough to do all of these things every day. The more open your culture is, the less blame shifting and finger pointing there will be.

At the heart of everything, stamping out we/theyism is about ownership. When everyone "owns" the organization, understands the financials, has input into decisions, and works to solve their own problems, a victim mentality cannot thrive. There can't really be a we/they problem when everyone is "we." There can't be winners and losers because everyone wins or loses together—leaders, employees, and ultimately, customers. It's just a healthier way to work and live.

24 Create a Culture of Ownership Inside Your Company

One of the questions CEOs, business owners, and leaders ask is "How can I get employees to act like owners?" To put it in somewhat simplistic terms, the answer is to treat them like owners. No question about it: the experience of being an owner *is* different from the experience of being an employee. But a well-run company creates an ownership culture, which can come pretty close to closing the gap between the two types of experiences.

Most of us have probably done business with companies that instill that sense of ownership as well as with those that don't. Here are two personal examples:

Example 1: I was hungry and really wanted something from a takeout place that was located about 10 minutes from where I lived at the time. It was 8:35 p.m. and the restaurant was open until 9 p.m. I pulled into the parking lot at about 8:45 p.m. When I got to the door I noticed it was locked and the two employees had the chairs on the tables and were cleaning up. Checking my watch and noting the hours on the door I knew I was there in time. I knocked softly. Then I knocked louder. I felt the workers could hear me, but they kept cleaning. So I drove home.

Because many of these stores are independently owned franchises, I know this experience may be an exception rather than the norm. However, I have never been back to that restaurant. My thinking: if the owner had been there, the door would have been open and I would have received my meal. Owners want to make customers happy.

Example 2: My wife, daughter, and I were driving home from a football game. It was about 8:55 p.m. and we realized we did not have much at home to eat, so we decided to find a spot. My daughter mentioned a restaurant that premakes pizzas to cook at home. Seeing the time, I said I doubt they can make us one, however, let's stop and see. When we walked in, I saw that the owner wasn't there. I apologized for getting there so near closing time and said, "I understand if we are too late." The employees on duty quickly said, "Not at all . . . what can we get you?"

While we were waiting, two more customers came in and they also got served. I was impressed. While serving customers who came in late may have cost a bit of overtime, no doubt the revenue covered the expenses. The pizza was great and we have gone back to this restaurant at other times and have shared the positive experience with others. Clearly, this business owner had created a culture of ownership.

There is a stark contrast between the mind-sets of these two sets of employees. I sometimes share these examples when speaking with organizations on the difference between "renting" and "owning."

During such sessions I'll ask: "Who currently rents where they live?" When someone in the crowd raises their hand, I will ask them a few questions:

- How much was the property you rent bought for?
- How much are the mortgage payments?
- How long is the mortgage?
- What is the interest rate?
- What does the landlord pay in taxes?

As one might expect, the person typically can't answer any of these questions. Why? Because landlords don't share that information with renters. This creates a very incomplete picture of the financials involved in property ownership. The same is true in the business world.

Here is the point: if we want employees to act like owners, we must not treat them like renters. Here are some tips that help to create a sense of ownership:

Be a model owner. Everyone watches you. People will follow your lead. Years ago, I knew the head of a residency program for physicians. He told me he wanted to see how much influence his actions had. Residents would round on patients, either as a group or with the director and other physicians. So the residency director started putting his hand on the patient's right shoulder as he talked with them. Sure enough, all the residents were soon doing the same. This is not unusual. Model the behavior you are looking for in others, particularly the mind-set. When you show them owner qualities like "every job is your job," you can get them on board with this thinking, and you can shift a culture very quickly.

Share the financials. Owners see the financials. Renters don't. Most times an employee sees the revenue coming in and assumes the owner is making lots of money. Most times employees do not realize the expenses an owner incurs beyond the obvious. They may not understand, for example, why there is no overtime. Or (and this is even worse) they may go to the other extreme and assume the owner/company isn't doing well. At that point they might look to jump ship or help create rumors that the business is in trouble. This creates even more problems.

Sharing financials with an explanation creates ownership. People will better understand the decisions you make and will be more likely to cooperate. I learned this when working at a place that was experiencing serious financial challenges. To help the staff realize what was going on, all financials were shared. We showed in black and white what expenses needed to be based on current revenues. Immediately, we had much improved behavior in cost management and service. Later, when I became a president of an organization, I used this experience and shared all financial data with employees.

Regularly solicit employee input. Share the problems. Let them help set goals. Ask for help in product development, marketing, product selection, and so forth. Owners are involved in the decision-making process. Ask the employees for their insights and opinions on all aspects of operations. In addition to asking basic questions like, "What do you think?" go deeper. Ask "What are the downsides of the idea/product?" "What will it take to be successful?" "What am I missing?"

If it's at all feasible to incorporate employee suggestions, it is often good to do so. It shows them that you are serious about wanting their input. Even if you may not agree with every employee every time, it gets important subjects out in the open, which leads to good conversations. And it gets employees in the habit of thinking like owners.

Have staff weigh in on hiring coworkers. Owners hire. So let the staff hire with you. Involve the employees who will be working with or for a candidate in the interview process. Make sure coworkers, not the owner independently, have the ultimate "yes" or "no" on hiring. Making them part of the selection process creates ownership and makes them feel more responsibility for the new hire's success as well.

While business owners may feel the heat to quickly get someone in place, coworkers may be more selective on who will be a good fit. They will not support the hiring of anyone they feel will not pull their own weight. They will even say "let's wait and work short rather than hire the wrong person." Employees will also be very helpful to the new person *so long as* they are part of the hiring decision.

Be careful not to be a full-time park ranger. What do I mean by this? Basically, insist that people solve their own problems. What I call Park Ranger leadership is the attitude that leaders will swoop down and rescue employees if they get "lost in the wilderness." This has always been a challenge for companies but as the business world has become more and more complex it just isn't feasible anymore. It's not humanly possible for leaders to have all the answers.

Ask that when employees bring a problem they also bring a solution. Tell them because they are closer to the problem they are well suited to come up with a practical and workable fix. Even if the solution ends up not working, it may be a good starting point, and it will definitely send the message that people own their jobs and the issues that come with them. Soon employees will start to think like entrepreneurs, which frees leaders up to do their own work. When this happens in every department it quickly leads to a more innovative and resilient organization.

Regularly connect employees back to the *why* behind their work. This goes deeper than "to make money" or even "to help the company make money." When the company is stronger, jobs are more secure, which means a better life for workers and their families. And if you take it a step further, the more prosperous workers are, the more it strengthens the entire community. The *why* also connects to the customer's quality of life. Employees make life better for customers by preparing a great meal for them, or building a car they'll love driving, or providing them with an insurance policy that gives them peace of mind for their future.

The more you can help the employee see and connect emotionally to the role they play in the customer's life, the more responsible they'll feel for that customer's satisfaction and experience. This is what ownership looks like.

My experience is that employees will act like owners when they are treated like owners. CEOs or business owners sometimes worry about taking these steps—especially sharing the financials. Yet, after it is done the response is usually "I wish I had done this sooner." The fact is that creating and sustaining a culture of ownership creates a better company. It's just one more step on the journey to making life better for employees, customers, and the community.

25

Mentors Matter:

Here's How to Be One and How to Work with One

L eaders are always looking for ways to build the skill set of their employees and improve engagement. Putting a formal mentoring program in place may be one of the most cost-effective and efficient ways to help transfer knowledge from more experienced employees to those who want and need additional training. Great mentoring programs are the kind of personal development people want. They will help you attract and retain talent and leverage your most valuable asset—your people.

Mentorship is a partnership between individuals to promote professional and career development. The key word is *partnership*. A mentor must be an active participant in the relationship. The ideal mentee is a motivated individual who is open to feedback, coaching, and guidance. They also need the ability to learn, a good dose of patience, and comfort with being a team player. Both parties must be highly engaged, so making participation in a mentoring program mandatory probably won't work.

Mentoring has many benefits. Mentees learn practical skills they can use on the job and gain insight into the organization's culture and the nuances of the company. The organization gains more highly skilled leaders and employees and creates a more positive and engaged workplace. Mentoring helps build relationships and can be a great way to get honest feedback and figure out what employees are passionate about (all key to reducing turnover). It's a great way to show the company cares. Mentors enjoy the many rewards of "giving back" and also gain leadership and coaching skills and learn other things from the process.

If your company has a formal mentorship program, great. Many don't. But as a leader you can always take the initiative to offer your mentoring services to someone, find a mentor for yourself, or connect potential mentors and mentees with each other.

There are certain qualities and behaviors that make someone a great mentor. Whether you're serving as a mentor or seeking one out, here is what "great" looks like:

Great mentors have done it and/or are doing it. They are respected in their organizations and in the community.

Great mentors are willing to share their knowledge, expertise, and skills. They understand where the mentee is, they relate to the time when they were there themselves, they show sincerity, and they freely give away what they have learned.

But they don't just give the answers. Instead, they help the mentee arrive at the answers. Great mentors want mentees to think for themselves. They listen fully and ask probing questions. They understand their job is simply to enhance and awaken the best part of you. They believe the skill, the courage, and the confidence are there; they just need to release it. Sometimes they ask mentees to go away and think about an issue for a while and report back.

They focus on character at least as much as skill. They know that values, self-awareness, integrity, and empathy matter more than knowing how to perform tasks. A mentee can always learn how to do something. Guidance on how to be will serve them better in the long run.

Great mentors aren't afraid to get personal. They know there is no sharp divide between work life and personal life. It's a real relationship. Sometimes the lines get blurred and that's okay.

Great mentors walk the walk. They live by the same behaviors they are teaching.

They are honest about their shortcomings. If a mentor isn't yet where they want to be in their career and life, they say so. Mentors are human and not perfect. It is not fair to a mentor or a mentee for the mentor to be put on a pedestal.

Great mentors know they are not finished products. They have committed themselves to ongoing learning. They admit when they are still learning in the mentor–mentee relationship. They will often learn right along with the mentee.

Great mentors care. They take the role of a mentor seriously. They're like a guide on a mountain climb: they want to make sure the tools and skills are in place. They are committed to the mentee's success.

They are positive by nature. Mentors are cup-half-full people who help the mentee see the opportunities when facing obstacles. The mentee can feel the enthusiasm of the mentor, both spoken and unspoken.

They help the mentee hold up the mirror. They provide constructive feedback and guidance. Mentors help the mentee leverage their strengths. A mentor will also benefit from the lessons as it will help them hold up their own mirror.

Great mentors teach from experience. They do not ask a mentee to take steps they themselves did not take. They share their own self-awareness and development plan and their own goals.

They demand accountability. If the mentee isn't living up to their end of the bargain or if they otherwise aren't doing their best, a great mentor is willing to say so. They tend to have some structure around meeting times, goals, expectations, and milestones.

They also help the mentee find other mentors. Even the best mentor will also have gaps in their knowledge. They don't mind admitting this. Due to their experience and network, they have a lot of social capital and can usually connect the mentee with other resources. In addition, they should know how much they can help and when it's time to get someone else involved.

Great mentors tell the hard truths (but they do it with caring). They explain that even when feedback is not positive, it is because they care and are committed to the mentee's success. They connect to the why. And when tempers flare, which sometimes happens, they are patient with the mentee.

These are really just tips I've collected over the years. I know there are many more out there. If you're thinking of becoming a mentor, consider doing some research. There are great resources out there for setting up a very effective program. Being a mentor is work. Be sure to reward and recognize those in your organization who are willing to give their time to the effort.

How to Be a Great Mentee

Now, let's talk briefly about the other party in this relationship: the mentee. Anyone, no matter how experienced they are, can benefit from being a mentee—particularly if they are entering a new field or taking on an ownership role for the first time.

If you are a mentee looking for a mentor, do some research. Then, list three to five people who may fit what can help you most. After that, just ask. You'll be surprised at how many would say yes.

Some may decline when asked and that's okay. Don't take it personally. There could be good reasons for some to say no, like family, health, and so on. Many will be surprised you asked them because they may be selling themselves short on the impact they are making and the impact they could have on a mentee. While it's great if they work inside your company, that might not always be possible. You may find someone who is a better fit somewhere else.

The ideal mentee is a motivated individual who is open to feedback, coaching, and guidance. They also need the ability to learn, as well as patience and to be comfortable with being a team player.

Here are a few tips for being a good mentee:

Clearly communicate needs. As one might assume, ambiguity can make a mentor/mentee much less effective. It's important for a mentee to communicate the most pressing needs clearly and in a timely manner so the mentor can help.

Share thoughts, worries, fears, and hopes for the future. That's what a mentor is for. A good mentee is honest about where they are and where they stand. Even the best mentor can't really help if they don't know the truth. Offer both short- and long-range plans.

Get familiar with the mentor's background. What strengths do they bring to the table? A mentor can have decades of experience that can be vitally important to a newcomer's success. Perhaps their strength isn't to be able to provide financial backing. Understanding the background and skill set a mentor has will help maximize the guidance they can provide.

Take ownership of the relationship. It's important for the mentee to own the communication. Setting up meetings and phone calls keeps the relationship alive. One effective way would be to prepare a meeting agenda in advance to keep the conversation productive and on task. Be mindful of the mentor's time.

Be self-aware. Identify specific areas in which you know you need improvement and work on them. Be humble, willing to learn, and curious. Few people want to mentor a know-it-all.

Do the work. Come early, stay late, go the extra mile, and show a real commitment to getting better. Watching your growth and development is fulfilling to mentors.

A mentor is there to develop, but it can affect the relationship negatively if the mentor finds him- or herself working harder at the mentee's success than the mentee is. Identify and execute.

Ask for feedback. Don't wait for the mentor to provide it. For example: "What questions should I be asking that I have not asked?" and "On a scale from 1 to 10, with 10 being highest, rate my follow-up actions since we last met."

One of my favorite sayings is, "When the student is ready, the teacher appears." A good mentee stays ready and looking for the right mentor to appear, so that when the right person comes along, they are able to fully capitalize on it.

A better-trained, more engaged workforce is what everyone wants. A good mentorship program can help you achieve this. Start small if you need to, but get something underway. You won't believe what a game changer it can be.

26 Reducing Workplace Drama:

How It Harms Your Company and How to Shut It Down

From time to time, most of us have experienced or even contributed to workplace drama. It can take many different forms: people gossip, spread rumors, complain, lash out emotionally, rant about a perceived wrong, purposely exclude others, take sides in conflicts, and so forth. No matter how drama manifests, it can be a highly destructive force inside a company.

Drama contributes to a less professional workplace. It creates bad feelings and lowers morale. It keeps people from being able to work together effectively. It tears teams apart. For all of these reasons, workplace drama hurts productivity. Ultimately, it creates the kind of culture that drives away high performers and keeps you from attracting great talent.

We need to realize that those who create workplace drama aren't always doing it intentionally. Sometimes their behavior is driven by insecurity, fear, or other undealt-with emotional issues. But in most cases I believe drama stems from people not knowing how to handle conflict. I get it. Facing conflict head on and having tough conversations with people isn't easy or comfortable for anyone. Yet it's crucial for leaders to know how to do both. (See Chapters 13 and 14 for more on these subjects.)

Great leaders take a zero-tolerance stance against drama. Their behavior and their words let employees know they value a drama-free environment where people cultivate healthy, respectful, collaborative adult relationships. Here are a few tips:

Model the behavior you want to see. Don't participate in drama yourself. Don't gossip or badmouth anyone. Strive to always be aboveboard, fair, respectful, and positive. Be really careful about even small things: for example, copying someone you don't need to copy on a sensitive email. Never stop examining your own motives and hold yourself to the highest standard. The leader *always* sets the tone for workplace behavior. If it's okay for you to do it, employees assume it's okay for them. Be aware of the messages you're sending.

Have a system for managing conflict. Train employees on how situations should be resolved and give them specific steps for getting there. In many cases, they may not realize how harmful their actions are. With just a little training and expectation setting, you can eliminate many of the problems.

Be as transparent as possible. Drama thrives in secretive environments. This is one of many reasons why it's a good idea for organizations to be open about everything from financials to performance metrics to changes that might be coming in the future. The less people have to speculate about, the less likely they'll be to gossip and repeat hearsay. Leaders need to be transparent, too. The less you have to hide, the less you'll have to worry about who you told and whether they will repeat it.

Ask for specificity. When people make blanket statements like "everybody says" and "everybody thinks," ask them for names and particulars. Who is *everybody*? I have found in my work with communities that when people start using generalities like this to build a case for their position (usually a negative one), they can typically only name one or two people. They are creating a lot of emotion without a lot of substance behind it. Forcing specificity helps us put issues in perspective and shuts down drama.

Stop repeating the story. Encourage employees to keep the story in the group that needs to hear it. When something happens that gets people upset they may feel the need to tell their story over and over. Usually this is because they want support or attention. As leaders we need to be careful not to do this ourselves and we need to let employees know how destructive this can be. When we

repeat stories over and over they become larger than life and perpetuate negativity throughout the organization.

Hold open conversations about real issues. When there is an issue, the goal is to get it fixed, not go behind people's backs and
complain. Far better to approach the person and have an open conversation. Back up your statement with data. For example: "In the
past month you have missed three deadlines. Can we talk about
what the problem might be?" Often, addressing the issue openly
will help you uncover a root cause. Once you zero in on the factor
keeping the employee from doing their job properly, you can work
with them to find a solution.

Encourage people to carry their own messages. If an employee
comes to you complaining about a third party—whether it's a
fellow employee or an immediate supervisor—ask, "Have you
spoken to this person directly?" A big part of creating an ownership mind-set is teaching employees to work out their own
conflicts and advocate for themselves rather than "telling on"
people. Remember, the goal is always adult relationships. Adults
resolve their own issues rather than stirring up drama.

Try to understand people's motivations. Sometimes an employee may create drama unintentionally. Their motive might be
pure but their delivery or process is broken. Maybe they really
do need something fixed but don't know how to go through the
proper channels to get it done. Usually by having a probing conversation with the person, you'll be able to figure out their motivation. You can then use it as a teachable moment, explaining
how they might better handle similar situations in the future.

Shut down troublemakers immediately. If you see that someone
is intentionally engaging in bad behavior or stirring up trouble,
take a two-pronged approach. First, don't join in the conversation
the troublemaker has started. Stay professional and aboveboard.
Next, narrate to the troublemaker (and everyone) that drama is un-
acceptable. Reiterate the kind of environment you are trying to create inside your company. Sometimes we all need a gentle reminder.

Extend grace. Let people back in the fold. If someone has made a
mistake, give them another chance. Don't hold a grudge or, worse,
turn the company against them. We're all human and we all have
bad moments and bad days. In general, discourage self-righteous
or "I'm done here!" attitudes that assume the worst of people and

make it okay to give up on them. Recognize the humanity and fallibility of others. In your words and actions, demonstrate that extending a little grace to people when they stumble is a good thing.

Reward and recognize people who get it right. We all learn by example. For instance, when you see someone handling conflict in a positive way, thank them and acknowledge them publicly. Likewise, admit it when you get it wrong. If you do something that creates or perpetuates drama, own it and apologize. People respect leaders who are vulnerable and honest about their flaws.

Few workplaces will ever be 100 percent drama-free. Human beings have shortcomings and get carried away by emotions. Yet I believe that the vast majority of people truly want good things for their coworkers and their company. When they realize how destructive drama can be, and learn more productive ways to get their needs met, they will work hard to change for the better and create a stronger, more positive culture and a higher-performing organization.

27 Make an Effort to Become a Millennial-Friendly Leader

There are plenty of stereotypes floating around about Millennials. Many of these are negative. Yet in working with businesses and communities around the country I've gotten to know many of these young people and have found that these stereotypes are not always accurate. I have coached and worked with many Millennials, and I like, respect, and value the vast majority of these young people.

Millennials aren't a separate species. While they can be different from their older counterparts in many ways, generational differences are often overstated. Many of them can also be attributed to simple age differences between younger workers and older workers. Any challenges you notice might be a matter of experience, not evidence of a generational paradigm shift.

So yes, as a group, Millennials have some shared characteristics due to being born in the same era, but that is true of every generation. Realistically, when a person was born doesn't define their work ethic or personality, nor does it mean they are all the same. Individual Millennials are just like individual Baby Boomers and Generation Xers— we're all unique with our own set of strengths and challenges. We all deserve to be considered on our own merits.

That said, we older leaders need to seek to understand Millennials and leverage their gifts and their know-how (and they have plenty of both). Besides, they are the largest group in the workforce (Pew Research puts them at 35 percent) and are expected to make up more than 50 percent of all workers by 2020.[1, 2] You need the energy of this group!

Who are Millennials anyway? They are the individuals who were born in the 1980s and 1990s. The oldest Millennial is now 39, while the youngest is 19. Here are a few of the traits generally ascribed to this group:

■ They grew up with technology and know how to use it. (We need this knowledge!)
■ They tend to look past "established thinking" and be more innovative and entrepreneurial.
■ They are adaptive and will grow well with proper leadership.
■ They are generally more connected with their emotional well-being, and value and thrive in a positive atmosphere.
■ They love diversity and work toward inclusion.

As you can see, these are incredibly positive attributes and skills and behaviors every organization would love to have! (Why do so many of us focus on negative generalizations instead of positive ones?) The key to being a Millennial-friendly leader is understanding this group of talented young people and knowing how to leverage their unique qualities. Here are a few tips:

Don't stereotype them. As mentioned earlier, while there are some characteristics that seem common across the board, not all Millennials are the same. Don't go into the relationship with firm expectations about how they will or won't act. Keep an open mind and watch to see how their talents and abilities present themselves.

Yes, **they are very tech-friendly. Take advantage of that!** Millennials can help modernize and automate your company. Don't wait for them to offer—ask them what high-tech updates they recommend. Use them as a resource to improve your own tech savviness; even if they find your "old school" ways amusing they will most likely be delighted to help you learn. Let them know that you value their ability to use technology. Everyone likes to feel valued and appreciated.

It's true: Millennials can move around rather quickly. Don't be afraid of turnover (or punish them for leaving). The gig economy is real. Our understanding of what a career looks like (or should look like) is quickly evolving. Millennials are not afraid to change jobs, and their employers shouldn't be afraid of it either.

Don't be afraid of having to replace them, but also be careful to manage them and the company in such a way that no one person is essential to the operation.

Millennials value learning and growth. Train them well. They judge a job by what they're learning, not what they're making. Understand that they are not going to be there forever, and give opportunities for professional development and continuing education that will serve them well in their current role and also move them forward wherever they go in the future. Putting this training infrastructure in place will serve everyone well!

Have a good policy in place for remote workers. Autonomy and scheduling flexibility are important to this group, so the option to work remotely will be a big plus (even if it's just a few days a week). This policy will help you attract and keep the best and the brightest, not just with Millennials, but with other groups as well. Organizations designated as "Best places to work" routinely allow employees to work virtually, and an increasingly large number of people are doing so. While employees love working remotely, it is proving to be good for employers, too, in terms of both cost savings and productivity.

Give them honest feedback. This generation wants to grow. Tell them how. Don't be afraid to give the truth, positive or negative, but tell them how to improve.

Collaboration is key. Look for opportunities for Millennials to work on cross-functional teams. Not only will this help them feel more connected to their colleagues, it also exposes them to a different skill set and gives the opportunity to learn about functions that are outside of their current role. For a generation that is expected to change jobs (and careers) more than any that came before them, this is a huge bonus.

They are less inclined to get complacent, but more likely to complain. Don't be offended when they get disgruntled and express it. Millennials have a totally different relationship with authority and respect. They may not always present feedback/suggestions to management in a positive tone. When this happens, be careful not to respond to their tone, but instead look at their message and evaluate whether what they're saying is true, valid, or useful. Just because they are disgruntled doesn't mean they are wrong. Sometimes the best ideas come from people who are just fed up with the status quo.

Listen to what they have to say. Millennials are a group that has something to say, and they want you to listen. Not only will this help them feel engaged, it will serve your company well. Millennials bring an interesting and new perspective that can be quite valuable. (We all have blind spots.) Besides, like any employee, if they don't feel listened to they are not likely to perform at their peak.

Figure out what motivates them and connect to it. Young people tend to be motivated by different things than older folks. It's not always about how much they take home at the end of the day. They might be motivated by leaders who connect their day-to-day work with a higher purpose, praise them for good work, or invest in their personal development. Figure out what their *what* is, and connect to it. (This is also true for employees of any generation.)

Have a coffee machine, hot tea station, and healthy snack options (and other perks that encourage productivity). Small workplace benefits like this matter to younger workers. They value the convenience, but more than anything they value what these small perks signify, which is that their leaders took a second to think about what they need, and did something to make their day better.

Know when to give freedom and when to give clear directions. It's often said that Millennials need "the freedom to perform." It's true that this group doesn't love being micromanaged, but they also value clear and firm instructions to follow, particularly on tasks that they might be unfamiliar with. Balancing these two approaches requires a soft touch. Know when to give flexibility, and when to set up rules and procedures that set them up for success.

They tend to be innovative and entrepreneurial. Don't demonize failure. Encourage vulnerability. Vulnerability is a huge buzzword right now, and it's partially because Millennials don't connect with idealized "perfect" leaders, or work well in situations that don't allow them to be their (imperfect) selves. Instead of forcing an unreachable standard of perfection, design metrics that reward risk taking, innovative thinking, and other actions that require vulnerability. Not only will it serve you well by bringing out good ideas, but it will also serve to make you much more popular with younger employees.

Be genuine. The best way to connect with young people is to simply be genuine, sincere, and authentic when dealing with them. Don't try to be something you are not. They will see through this. Be frank. Don't sugarcoat what you need to say—they tend not to soften their own messages and may view a leader's effort to do so with cynical eye.

Ask them how they are doing (and don't accept "fine" as an answer). It's important to engage emotionally with Millennials. They see your relationship not just as a work relationship but as a personal one. Don't be afraid to let them know you care.

Survey and measure them regularly so you can inspire them and chart growth. For example, measure their strengths and weaknesses so that they know where they shine and where they could use more development. This way you can reframe praise in light of their strengths and provide them with tools to help compensate for their weaknesses. For example, if you know that they require a lot of personal praise, you might consider validating them based on how the team performs instead of their personal performance. Or if you know they are forgetful, you can teach them how best to keep and use a list.

Finally, take a hard look at what your company stands for. What is your mission? How do you make the world a better place? As a group Millennials care deeply about corporate social responsibility. They want to buy from and work for companies that are good corporate citizens and they want to feel like they are a part of something bigger than themselves. Make sure your company is "giving back" in some way. Hopefully this is already true, but if not it may be time to step up your game. Being a values-driven company will make it easier to help young employees connect back to that sense of meaning and purpose that drives all humans to do their best work.

As you read through this list, you may start to see that these are things that nearly every employee wants. See? We aren't that different!

People tend to live up (or down) to our expectations. So much of what an employee, coworker, or colleague brings to a company depends on the messages you send them, how much time you spend training, coaching, and mentoring them, and how willing *you* are to learn from *them*. We get out of relationships only what we are willing to put in. So make an effort to see the very real gifts that Millennials bring to the table and get intentional about making full use of them. They can make your company better and stronger than ever before.

Notes

1. Richard Fry, "Millennials Are the Largest Generation in the U.S. Labor Force," *Fact Tank*, Pew Research Center, April 11, 2018, http://www.pew research.org/fact-tank/2018/04/11/millennials-largest-generation-us -labor-force/.
2. "Millennial Insights for the 2020 Labor Market," MRINetwork, January 5, 2017, http://www.mrinetwork.com/articles/industry-articles/millennial -insights-for-the-2020-labor-market/.

28

Be a Positive Ambassador for Your Organization— and Teach Others to Do the Same

Most of us have experienced how powerful it can be when an employee manages up a company and its products. We've all had a server say something like: "We're known for our incredible steaks. Our chef Marco is a master at cooking steaks and finding the perfect sides to pair with them. And you *must* try the fresh watermelon and feta salad!"

Or we've been in a clothing boutique and had a salesperson say: "Let me show you these new textured twill jackets we just got in. Elaina—that's our buyer—has a real gift for finding the best fabrics at the most reasonable prices. I am so excited to show these to my favorite customers!"

Chances are, you not only went with the recommended meal or purchased the jacket, you also felt good about your decision. And you probably felt great about the business, told your friends about it, and looked forward to coming back again. Now, imagine how amazing it would be if you and your employees represented the company this way all the time, 24/7.

You might be thinking, *Of course the server and the salesperson said good things about their company and product. They wanted to sell something.* Well, yes. That's the point. As leaders and employees we need to make it our business to *always* be "selling" the company, whether we're talking to a coworker, a customer, or even a friend outside work. Not in an overly promotional or manipulative way, but in an authentically positive one.

All of us, whatever our role or leadership status, need to think of ourselves as company ambassadors. It's in our best interest to share positivity, not cynicism. People are drawn to our company because they want to be part of something positive. If we honestly can't contribute to this kind of experience, we may need to ask ourselves why we are choosing to work here in the first place.

In my work with communities I find people can be negative at times about where they live. This always surprises me. I don't think people realize how damaging it is to verbally tear down their community. In many cases it's just a bad habit they've fallen into. But how can they expect to attract investors and great talent to make their community better if they don't have good things to say? And if that's how they feel, why are they choosing to live there?

This doesn't mean we shouldn't be aware of challenges and work to make improvements. Of course we should. But in general, we should be more focused on the positive aspects than the negatives and we should be eager to talk about them to others. What we say about our company actually plays a huge role in creating its brand.

In other words, we (leaders and employees) should always seek to manage up our company, the people who work there, and the customers who buy from us. Managing up simply means positioning others in the best possible light. Employees can manage up the boss, the boss can manage up employees, and everyone can manage up the organization. Managing up is a hugely important skill and you can't be a good ambassador without it.

So what *are* the benefits of being a good ambassador? Most obviously, when we manage up the company and its products and services it helps us make more sales. It helps customers feel less anxious about their purchase (especially if they're spending a lot of money) and they're more pleasant to deal with. All of this leads to repeat customers who refer others and who generate positive word of mouth.

When leaders manage up the company to employees, it reassures them that they are in a good place. It builds the brand in their mind. Not only does it help them feel good about working there, it gives them the language to manage up the organization to others.

Positive ambassadorship creates the kind of culture that attracts and retains great talent. High performers want to work where it's obvious that employees are thriving and happy. When potential job candidates hear employees saying great things about a company, they naturally want to be part of it. *Especially* at a time when talented people have lots of employment options, we all need to think of ourselves as recruiters.

Finally, being positive about your company just feels better—to you and to those you interact with, whether they're fellow employees, customers, or even strangers. People respond to positivity. It raises our energy, makes us happier and more pleasant to be around, draws others to us, improves our relationships, and opens the floodgates to greater creativity.

Here are some ways leaders can be a positive ambassador for your company and teach employees to do the same:

Be a world-class noticer. Look for things that are going well to manage up. Some opportunities to manage up are obvious. You can manage up the organization and its employees when you get a new client or hit a key goal. But train yourself to look for little day-to-day moments as well: when a customer praises a staff member, when someone stays late to finish a project, when a project team hits a tight deadline. Don't pass up an opportunity to accentuate the positive. Others may notice and start doing it, too, but don't count on that; make managing up part of your training. The idea is to get everyone in the habit so that it becomes a natural part of your culture.

Set the right example for employees. Ask yourself honestly: Do I send positive messages about the company? If not, vow to change that right now. Get in the habit of being your company's most vocal cheerleader. Frequently say how happy you are to be working there. Manage up coworkers and employees when you introduce them to others ("This is Michelle. She is the best accountant I've ever worked with!") and speak highly of them at all times. When you are consistently positive, employees will follow your lead.

Don't fake it. People can tell when you do. Instead, find authentic bright spots you can feel good about and focus on them. When I meet with a community or a business, I like to kick things off by asking them to focus on bright spots. What are the top three reasons they love their community? What are three reasons this is a great company to work for? They almost always come up with lots of examples and it really shifts the mood. This exercise always raises the energy level in the room and people immediately get in a creative and productive mind-set.

Teach employees to avoid the "we/they" trap. If you'll recall from Chapter 23, we/theyism occurs when we position ourselves in a positive light by making someone else the "heavy." An employee might say, "Sorry, the people in that branch are always slow to respond. I'll handle it for you!" Explain to employees that this may make a customer feel better about you but it will make them feel worse about the company. Far better to cheerfully take ownership of the situation and help the customer, and maybe offer an apology, without any negative commentary about anyone else. We need to function as a unified organization, not a divided one.

Make sure everyone is well-trained in sending the right messages to customers. Employees may fall back on practices like we/they and other bad habits simply because they've never been taught the *right* way to interact with customers. Give them the right tools and they'll say the right things. For example, teach them to manage up coworkers—and provide key words and phrases to use as appropriate—and to narrate processes so the customer always knows what's going on. If you give them the words, they will be much more likely to use them.

For example: "When we take your dog into the grooming salon we will give him a treat and allow him plenty of time to get acclimated. We only use safe, nontoxic shampoos and other products. Oh, and we always match each dog with a well-trained and professionally certified groomer experienced in working with that particular breed." Not only does all of this alleviate customer anxiety, it leaves the customer feeling good about your company.

Don't just *tell* employees to be good company ambassadors. Explain the "why." Usually when people understand the "why" they are far more likely to do what you're asking them to do. Help them connect the dots that when they speak positively about the company or manage up a coworker, and customers will be more pleasant to serve . . . and they'll make more sales . . . and the company will make more money . . . and they will have a more secure job. Don't assume they already know this. They may not—and even if they do, we all need a reminder at times.

Reward and recognize those who practice positive ambassadorship. This can be as simple as just saying publicly, "I'd like to thank

Marcus for representing our company so well. One of his regular customers, Mrs. Davidson, told me that she does business with us because he is always smiling and makes her feel like he and the company care about her as an individual." Recognized behavior gets repeated. Also, by drawing attention to high performers you encourage others to watch and emulate them.

You might consider asking the CEO to recognize high performers and positive ambassadors as well. This is a way of managing up the CEO and the employee simultaneously. The CEO feels good about the employee, the employee feels good about the CEO, and they both feel good about you. It's a win-win-win.

Emphasize the importance of managing up the company while off the clock as well. Tell employees: "When you're out in the community, be positive about your company and its products. People will hear what you say and they will remember." The truth is, you never know who is at the next table and what their connection might be to the company, a leader or coworker, or a client. Employees need think of themselves as representatives of the company and behave accordingly, 24/7.

Give them the tools to represent the company in public. For example, you might have tee shirts printed up with your company's name on them so employees can represent your brand outside of work. In fact, if you hold a competition where employees submit creative or funny designs, people will be more likely to want to wear them.

Make all employees unofficial salespeople. Encourage them to hand out business cards. You might also give them nice-looking promotional pieces to keep in their car "just in case," and you can help them develop a brief positive elevator speech about what your company does. When you arm people with tools they need to be positive ambassadors, they'll do it.

Teach employees to be very, very careful what they post on social media. Make it clear: even worse than venting in a public place is venting about the company on Facebook or any other social media site. (Even veiled negative statements like "Some people need to learn to appreciate their employees!" can be destructive.) Not only might the boss see an online rant, so might a customer or potential customer who just happens to Google your name.

158 The Busy Leader's Handbook

Most of us have good intentions. We don't go around badmouthing our boss, coworkers, or clients. But everyone can have a slip-up now and then if we're not careful. We need to always keep in mind that our company's future and our own future are intertwined. Not only should we refrain from saying negative things, we should look for opportunities to say good things.

When you look for ways to focus on the positive and to manage up others, you *will* find them. And they will ripple outward, creating more opportunities. Get in the habit of thinking this way and help employees do the same. If everyone in the company were to take just one small step toward being a positive ambassador, together we could make a huge difference in how our communities and customers see our company.

III Strategic/ Foundational Topics

This section focuses on the structure, processes, and practices that need to be hardwired if you're to build a successful organization. Together, these building blocks create a high-reliability culture that leads to consistent experiences for employees and customers alike. They drive decisions downward so that leaders can spend their valuable time working *on* the business, not *in* the business.

29 The Case for Structure:

Why Companies Should Hardwire Processes, Practices, and Other Foundational Building Blocks

Over the years I've seen too many leaders spend too much time working *in* their business rather than *on* their business. This is a serious problem. The real job of a leader is to work *on* the business—to define strategy, drive growth, and get the company to the next level. You need to spend your valuable time setting goals, tracking progress, making big-picture decisions, and building relationships. You *don't* need to be tied up in trenches working on day-to-day operations. These jobs need to be delegated to others.

When a leader gets stuck in the habit of working *in* the business they quickly create a situation where everything is dependent on them. This limits a company's growth. No single person, however driven or talented, can do everything! The solution is to put processes, procedures, and systems in place that give others a blueprint to follow. It's best to shore up these "building blocks" early on in your company's trajectory. However, no matter how long your company has been in business, it's not too late to define and shape them—or to revisit the ones you already have in place and make them better.

Standardizing and hardwiring processes and practices lets you create a high-reliability culture. This is something I learned in my healthcare career. High-reliability companies have very little variance, which is critical in life-or-death environments like hospitals. But really, every company should care about reducing variance in their products, services, and leadership. Why? Because it creates consistent experiences for employees, customers, vendors, and other stakeholders. Most people thrive in a culture of consistency and predictability.

When a company doesn't have strong structural building blocks in place, expectations are unclear. People don't truly know what the company stands for and what its goals are (even though leaders may assume they do). They don't know what their priorities are at any given time, nor do they know how they are being judged on their performance. They don't know how the company is performing. In fact, they, at times, may feel the company is doing well when it is not. Thus, they misread the bosses' sense of urgency.

This vagueness can paralyze employees. They feel they can't make decisions and must always get permission to act. As a result, things get bottlenecked at the top. If the leader isn't there, things can't move forward.

Beginning with a strong structural foundation drives decision-making downward because it creates clarity—and clarity is what most people crave. Knowing what the rules are and where the boundaries lie is empowering. It alleviates anxiety and makes it far easier to engage employees. It becomes obvious who is performing and who isn't and allows for fairness in how people are rewarded and recognized.

Leaders are able to spend less time putting out fires and solving problems and more time strategizing and growing the company. More things can roll on autopilot.

Standardizing and documenting the good practices and systems that create a company's foundation is the "fix" that heads off many problems that can cause it to struggle or even fail. What's more, it keeps the culture consistent as a company grows. When you come in and realize that you no longer know everyone in the room, at least you know what everyone in the room believes in regard to the company and their job.

This process might be a bit daunting, so here are a few tips that may help:

Take time to learn about the structural elements needed to build a strong company. We discuss some of the ones I feel are most important further in the pages of Section 3.

Think about who you're creating these systems and procedures for. Sure, *you* know the company inside and out but your staff may not. Keep your language very simple. Think through every detail. Break down all procedures into small, doable steps. Even if everyone knows it, write it down anyway. Over time, employees will come and go and having procedures documented will help with the transition.

Ask employees to help. They will appreciate being asked and will bring great value to the process. They probably have ideas for doing things that you never considered.

Don't be afraid to reinvent yourself. As you document your processes and procedures you will be forced to look closely at how you're doing things. You may see that some things you're doing don't make sense anymore. You might think of fresh ideas that evolve your business dramatically or take it in a whole new direction.

When you're ready to implement new processes, practices, or systems, take one thing at a time. Really get it down pat before moving on to the next one. It is easy for people to be so overwhelmed by too much change too fast that they become stuck in their own quicksand and move nowhere.

Review your practices and processes regularly. They are never set in stone. They will change as your company grows.

One more note: if you are the founder of your company, be aware that you may have a fundamental dislike of the idea of structure. This is typical of entrepreneurs. But structure is necessary if a company is to grow and thrive. In fact, authors and researchers Chip and Dan Heath say 80 percent of failures are from a lack of clarity. As we discussed earlier, structure brings clarity.

The greatest impediment to a company's long-term success is a lack of structure. If not put in place, eventually the company founder wears out, employees leave, customer service is inconsistent, and the needed revenue to sustain the company is not achieved. Yes, it takes time to build the foundation. However, a company that wants to achieve long-term success has no choice. *Run to structure, not away from it.*

Here are some of the key structural elements I recommend every company put in place:

- A mission statement, a vision statement, and identified values
- Clear goals that are communicated to all employees
- "Official" (written) standards of behavior
- A method for measuring the important things
- A leader development system (development for everyone in a supervisory role)
- A well-defined new employee selection process
- A plan for helping employees thrive in the first 90 days
- An employee training and development system
- An evaluation/job performance feedback system
- A way to measure employee engagement and customer satisfaction
- A well-run meeting system
- A way to collect and cascade best practices

In the next 12 chapters we'll cover each of the structural elements all companies need—brand new ventures, small businesses, and larger companies. No matter where your company is in its journey, make sure these key building blocks are in place as you move ahead.

30 Define and Live Your Mission, Vision, and Values

Your mission, vision, and values truly matter. This has always been true, but the subject is really in the spotlight right now. That's because we've moved into an era where people care more and more about working for (and buying from) companies that have a strong sense of purpose. As Millennials take over the workforce, being able to articulate why you exist, where you're going, how you make the world better, and what it means to work for you become even more important.

A World Economic Forum survey of young people found that more than 40 percent of them think sense of purpose/impact on society is one of their "most important criteria when considering job opportunities."[1]

What's more, another study of Millennials conducted by Cone Communications found that:

- 75 percent say they would take a pay cut to work for a responsible company (vs. 55 percent US average).
- 83 percent would be more loyal to a company that helps them contribute to social and environmental issues (vs. 70 percent US average).
- 88 percent say their job is more fulfilling when they are provided opportunities to make a positive impact on social and environmental issues (vs. 74 percent US average).[2]

Paying attention to your mission, vision, and values statements isn't just about making people feel good about working for you. And it's not just a "Millennials" thing, either. These guiding principles help define and communicate the all-important *why* that drives leaders and employees of all ages to do their best work. They connect us to the sense of meaning and purpose that engages people at every level, and engaged employees take a company from average to great.

Yet despite how important mission, vision, and values are to business performance, many leaders are confused by what these concepts mean. Here is an easy way to think about them:

The Mission is what the business actually does. It should be simple, factual, and to the point. A good mission statement will always bring decisions and actions back to the mission.

Here are a few examples of mission statements:

Google: To organize the world's information and make it universally accessible and useful.

Make-A-Wish: We grant the wishes of children with life-threatening medical conditions to enrich the human experience with hope, strength, and joy.

Life Is Good: To spread the power of optimism.

Your Vision expresses what you want to be in the future. It is an aspirational statement. It should be inspiring and connect to your employees' sense of meaning and purpose. Vision can and should drive the goals you set. For example:

IKEA: To create a better everyday life for the many people.

Oxfam International: Our vision is a just world without poverty.

If you're confused about the difference between mission and vision, just think about the difference between a "missionary" and a "visionary."

When you picture a missionary, it's the person on the ground, doing the day-to-day work of making the world a better place. It's highly operational.

A visionary, on the other hand, is a big picture "idea person" who might not be involved in the day-to-day operations, but who imagines a better world and guides their team in that direction.

Vision is what you want to accomplish; mission is how you get there.

The Values support the vision. They are the core beliefs everyone in the company should live by every day. I once heard it said that values don't just hang on the walls, they walk in the halls. I think that's a great description. Together your values become the guiding principle for the organization and the foundation for the standards of behavior for all leaders and staff to follow.

Here are some examples of values:

GoDaddy

- Extraordinary customer focus
- Own outcomes
- Join forces
- Work fearlessly
- Live passionately

Uber

- We build globally, we live locally.
- We are customer obsessed.
- We celebrate differences.
- We do the right thing. Period.
- We act like owners.
- We persevere.
- We value ideas over hierarchy.
- We make big bold bets.

If you aren't in love with your Mission, Vision, and Values statements, it may be time to revisit them. There are many articles out there on creating strong mission, vision, and values statements, so look around and see what resonates. Get key stakeholders involved. Reach out to fellow leaders, employees, and even customers and ask for input. Don't try to create these important guidelines sitting alone at the computer! The more points of view, the better. A business is a team sport and while everyone won't necessarily want to be involved in this exercise, everyone should at least have the chance to weigh in.

Mostly, I want to talk about values because they are the most granular expression of the first two statements. Research featured in Jim Collins's *Built to Last* examined companies that outlive their competitors. Values were shown to play a critical role in organizations attaining and sustaining success. (I imagine the same is true for people.)

Collins points out that every organization will face times when they must choose between profit and values. Those that chose profit found it helped in the short term, but in the long term they didn't do well. The companies that chose values took a short-term financial hit, but the research showed they run much better and last much longer.

For example, when Tylenol had a recall due to an issue in one isolated location, the company came out very quickly, communicated the issue, did a large recall, and took a similarly large financial hit. However, the company gained respect with how it handled the situation and it recovered financially.

Another example: a company's research and development team was working on an experiment with the potential for a highly profitable outcome. In the process, it stumbled upon another never-before-seen solution that wasn't profitable, but it could be a huge help to many third-world countries that could not pay the company. Did the company nix the unprofitable solution? No, it made the solution public for nothing. It chose values, something that could help the world, over profits. Today it is still a very successful company.

In most presentations, I close with a point about always bringing the changes we're asking employees to make back to values. Why? If an action connects with one's values, they will always take the action even if it is hard, they are tired, their team is short-staffed, or any other hurdle. The discomfort of *not* being true to one's values is worse than whatever action it takes to live the values. Even when it costs dollars, living the values is always the right decision.

I worked for an organization in the 1990s that received negative feedback on cleanliness. We had staff dedicated to cleaning and they worked hard, yet the customer service results still showed that too many customers felt the facility was not clean. All 1,500 employees decided to all take ownership of the situation and connected tactics of cleanliness to our organizational values of teamwork and stewardship.

We were immediately all on the environmental service team. If anyone saw any trash on the floor outside on the ground it was picked up. We learned that black scuffmarks on the tile could be taken off with the wiggle of a foot. We even jokingly called it the "organizational shuffle." A few months later our cleanliness results were some of the best in the nation. It wasn't just picking up litter. It was about living the company values. This experience has stuck with me to this day. I pick up litter both at work and wherever I am. We are stewards of our environment.

Values are both taught and caught. When you reinforce them and live by them, so will those around you. The more transparent you are about your company's mission and vision—and the clearer you are about how employees should live it every day—the more connected to the big picture they'll be. From this connection will flow engagement, greater passion, a sense of purpose, hard work, and ultimately, a thriving organization.

For some practical tips on how leaders can hardwire values into the organization, please see Chapter 5.

Notes

1. Shakir Akorede, "Here's What Millennials Really Want from Business, and Why," World Economic Forum, September 12, 2017, https://www.weforum.org/agenda/2017/09/heres-what-millennials-really-want-from-business/.
2. "2016 Cone Communications Millennial Employee Engagement Study," Cone Communications, November 2, 2016, https://static1.squarespace.com/static/56b4a7472b8dde3df5b7013f/t/5819e8b303596e3016ca0d9c/1478092981243/2016+Cone+Communications+Millennial+Employee+Engagement+Study_Press+Release+and+Fact+Sheet.pdf

31 Set Big, Bold, Clear Goals and Communicate Them to All Employees

Shoot for the moon, even if you miss you'll land among the stars.
· —*Norman Vincent Peale*

Gentlemen, we will chase perfection, and we will chase it relentlessly, knowing all the while we can never attain it. But along the way, we shall catch excellence.
· —*Vince Lombardi*

Goal setting seems easy enough. Set a goal, get it done. But we all know it's not really that easy. And that knowledge can lead us to aim pretty low. In fact, I recently read about an organization that set a fairly low goal of improvement. The leader went on to explain that they set the goal low so they could achieve it.

Think about that! Will the "setting goals low on purpose" approach truly achieve what leaders want? Probably not. So why do companies and their leaders set all-too-achievable goals, or worse yet, no goals at all?

Sometimes leaders don't set goals because they are so busy trying to manage the day-to-day workload that they barely have time to think about the future and what they want from it. They are in survival mode. Yet goals are important. Without them we drift aimlessly without a motivating sense of purpose. Goal setting is how you get intentional about accomplishing your vision.

In other cases leaders may set goals but stick with modest ones. Perhaps they had set lofty goals previously, and when those goals were not reached, they were criticized for not achieving them (even though they did show good improvement). All too often that's when the "playing it safe" goal is born. And that's too bad because lackluster goals are not good for organizations.

Jim Collins demonstrated that the best companies and companies that became great set what he termed "BHAGs." BHAG stands for *Big Hairy Audacious Goals*. While that goal was not always achieved, or maybe took a while to achieve, the organizations that set BHAGs did better than ones that did not set such goals.

I learned the value of setting big goals from Mark Clement, my former boss and a hospital CEO in Chicago, Illinois, in the mid-1990s. Mark had taken the role after the hospital had a significant layoff, lost around $7 million, and was struggling in many performance areas. One day at an executive team meeting the agenda was to set goals for the next year in several areas: quality, employee turnover, patient satisfaction, profit (as in let's *have* some profit this time), and so forth.

We started with patient satisfaction. Our rating was dismal, with a satisfaction percentile in the single digits nationally. Considering our terrible rating, we suggested the goal be the 50th percentile: just get to average. And even then the senior leader team was worried we had gone too far.

But Mark disagreed. "I'm not taking the goal of being average to our board," he told us.

So, we slowly raised the goal number to the 75th percentile and finally Mark was satisfied. I was told by the company measuring these satisfaction ratings that this kind of jump would be extremely difficult. Still, Mark shared this lofty goal with the board of directors and off we went.

With the goal so far from our current state, it quickly became apparent we would have to do things much differently. So, we did. We learned from others. We made a big effort to connect people to the "why"—meaning, why patient satisfaction was important and why we should make our company a better place to work for employees.

We missed the 75th percentile that next year. Instead, we made the 92nd percentile.

I firmly believe if we had left that meeting with the goal as the 50th percentile, we wouldn't even have reached that. Setting a high goal created an urgency to change and change quickly. Why? The patients deserved the best care. That is what the mission said.

That lesson followed me a few years later when I became the administrator of Baptist Hospital in Pensacola, Florida. During my first meetings with employees I shared that our goal needed to be to become the best hospital in the country.

"Do you mean *county*?" one employee asked. I clarified that no, I meant *country*—nation—the United States. Did we get there? In a few areas, but not every area. Still, we were better because of a lofty goal.

We learn from many others. Martin Luther King Jr. set lofty goals in civil rights. While we still have a long way to go, would we be further along if he had set low goals? I doubt it. President Kennedy said we would get to the moon. This lofty goal, like Dr. King's, inspired people.

If setting BHAGs is too much for you then set a milestone goal, then set stretch goals with a timeline. Just don't shy away from lofty goals, whether they are personal, work, home, or striving to make our community better.

A few goal-setting tips:

First, don't set too many goals. Remember, we have limited time and focus. When we set too many goals—say, more than seven or eight—we can't give each goal the attention it deserves. This is especially true when we're setting BHAGs, each of which will require a substantial amount of energy. Also, be realistic about timelines. Some goals can't be achieved in a year. They may take two or three years.

Be sure goals are aligned with your mission and vision. That way the sense of meaning and purpose—which is needed in order to inspire people put forth the extra effort—will be built right in.

Make the goals very specific, objective, and metrics-based. Goals should not be stated as: "We're going to improve our customer satisfaction scores" or "We're going to start a blog." They should be more like "We're going to move our customer satisfaction scores from 50 percent to 75 percent" or "We're going to write 15 blog posts a month."

Put one person in charge of each goal. (If everyone owns the goal, no one owns it and it won't get done.) Make sure meeting that goal is linked to their performance evaluation. It's even better if you can assign a "weight" to each goal so the responsible person will know how important it is to focus on in the grand scheme.

Check back in regularly to hold the person accountable for the goal. As we discuss in Chapter 38, performance evaluation systems work best when you hold quarterly reviews. That way you can ensure that the person responsible for a goal is making progress toward it. If they are not on track to meet the goal they'll know early in the year and will have time to course correct, receive more training, or whatever it takes to improve performance in this area.

Communicate goals company wide. Whether you have 5 employees or 100 (or more), everyone should know what the goal is and their individual role in meeting it. Clarity and transparency are essential if you're to engage people and create ownership. Remember, everyone plays a role in reaching goals. If your goal is to improve cleanliness, it doesn't just fall on janitorial staff. It falls on everyone.

Constantly and consistently connect back to the *why*. Why do you want to meet this goal? How will the company benefit? How will the customer benefit? I have found that most people truly want to do the right thing. When leaders do a good job communicating the reason for the goal they will step up and make the effort.

If you don't achieve a goal, evaluate why. Keep digging until you find a root cause—maybe there is a flaw in one of your processes or maybe key people need additional training in a specific area. Use the missed goal as an opportunity to refine and perfect your organization.

Goal setting matters because it drives people to put forth effort, improve performance, and generate more revenue for the company. But it also matters because it drives personal growth.

Zig Ziglar said, "What you get by achieving your goals is not as important as what you become by achieving your goals." I believe that. Goals empower us to become the best we can be not just as leaders or employees, but as human beings. When we're betting on ourselves we need to think big. We're worth the effort.

32 Put "Official" (Written) Standards of Behavior in Place

There is no single rule about what's acceptable in the workplace and what isn't. It varies across industries and from one company to another. Also, the "rules" change over time. Twenty years ago, it made sense for a company to prohibit mobile phone use during work hours. Now, almost everyone wants and expects to have access to their phone. Plus, individuals have different backgrounds and expectations—what's normal and acceptable to one person may not be to another.

For all of these reasons, if you don't spell out what good behavior looks like, everyone may not know. And yes, there may occasionally be that person who does know what good behavior is but for whatever reason chooses not to practice it. The solution is to get the entire company involved in developing a "Standards of Behavior" contract.

This document can address any and all aspects of behavior at work: from how we interact with clients and customers to the nitty-gritty of how we behave toward leaders and coworkers. If we can't help a customer do we find someone who can? Do we complain about problems or do we work to fix them? Do we come to meetings on time? Do we talk too loudly on the phone? Do we pitch in when a coworker needs help? All of these behaviors—and many others—can be spelled out and standardized.

If this seems extreme, consider just how important workplace behavior is. I find that when people are on their best behavior they communicate more clearly, there are fewer unpleasant conversations, and everyone enjoys being at work more. People work better in teams, which leads to better collaboration and innovation. And all of this together adds up to more engaged employees, improved performance and productivity, and yes, happier customers.

Consistency across the organization is the most elusive item in most companies. Some people may behave well all the time, others don't. Customers may have good things to say about one department but not another. Standards of behavior create a more consistent experience for everyone. Obviously, that's better for customers but it also feels better for employees. When times get tough economically it's good for morale to have a workplace that feels calm and stable.

Plus, people just do better when we are 100 percent clear on what the rules and boundaries are and when we see that everyone is following them. Blurred lines and vagueness make us anxious. Clarity sharpens our focus.

Because standards of behavior are written down and "official," they seem more real and people take them more seriously. Plus, once the standards are agreed upon and signed by everyone from the CEO on down, you'll have something official to hold people accountable to. This document truly does keep people on their toes and more aware of their behavior.

Managers will appreciate having firm guidelines to hold employees to. It makes their job easier, and makes it easier to recognize those who are doing it right and move out those who are consistently getting it wrong. "Shape up or ship out" conversations are much less ambiguous when everyone agrees on what the standards are, and understands why they are in place. It also allows employees an opportunity to have the "is this really a fair expectation?" conversation *before* something goes wrong.

Here are a few tips for creating and applying the standards:

Start by looking at your company's long-term objectives. Then, figure out which behaviors can help you meet them. What do you want to achieve over time? Where do you need improvement? Maybe your company has a goal of increasing repeat business. And maybe your customer satisfaction survey shows that customers who call in with a problem feel like they're rushed off the phone. So you might create a standard that anytime an employee talks to a customer they end the call or interaction by saying, "Are you having any other problems with our product or service that you'd like to tell me about? I have time."

Be very specific in your wording. (Remember, clarity counts.) In other words, don't write "Be polite to coworkers." That could be interpreted to mean almost anything. Instead, spell it out for employees. Write "Say thank you when someone helps you." Or "Say good morning when you pass someone's office as you arrive at work." Don't just write "No gossiping." Instead, write "Only say things about a leader or coworker that you would say directly to their face."

Spell out behaviors that show a strong commitment to leaders and coworkers. For example:

"I will discuss issues directly with coworkers rather than going to other people."

"I will respond promptly to all forms of communication."

"I will do everything possible to meet deadlines."

Include behaviors that impact the customer experience. For example:

"I will introduce myself to clients and customers and tell them my job title and experience—for example, 'I've worked here for five years and have become an expert in _____'" (fill in the blank with the service the client/customer is there for).

"I will address customers by name as soon as I hear it or see it in writing."

"If I cannot help a customer I will find someone else who can."

"I will ask customers to tell me if I am not meeting their expectations."

Before you finalize the document, give employees the final sign-off. Make sure everyone has a chance to review it and give their input as it's passed around for signing. If someone objects to a standard, listen to their concerns and alter it if you can. This makes buy-in a lot more likely. Plus, employees may come up with standards that you may never have thought of, just because they work "in the trenches" and know what the issues are.

Explain the "why" behind the Standards. Connect them to your mission, vision, and values. You may want to do an official roll-out to introduce the Standards. Whether you make a celebration out of it or just share it over your company's intranet, reinforce the reasoning behind them. For example: "Our mission is to be the best organic coffee shop in town. A big part of that is making customers feel at ease and at home. We also know that starts with a positive, happy, fun company culture. So, as you know, we've worked with the entire team to develop a set of behavior standards to help us all better meet these goals." When you explain the why and connect it to your larger purpose people won't feel a big list of rules is being "imposed" on them.

Have everyone sign the pledge to make it official. This includes the CEO. Just the act of putting pen to paper makes people far more likely to take the contents of a document seriously.

Use the standards to weed out unsuitable employees. Have candidates read and sign the standards even before you interview them. This gives people the chance to opt out if they don't feel your corporate culture is right for them. Two, if you do hire them, they'll know right away what you expect from them and will be able to get started on the right foot.

Give the document "teeth." If someone violates a standard, hold them accountable, even if it's just a matter of saying, "Remember, our Standards of Behavior says we'll return phone calls within 24 hours. It's been four days and you still haven't called Mr. Smith back." I have found most times a reminder is all it takes and there's usually no need to write people up or take more drastic measure. Most people want to do the right thing but we are all human.

If you violate a standard, admit it and apologize. The standards are for everyone, including leaders, and this is an opportunity to demonstrate that.

Treat the Standards of Behavior as a living document. Make changes as needed. As companies evolve and environments change, your standards of behavior may need to evolve, too. You might discover that one of the behaviors isn't working as intended, or you might discover that a new one needs to be added. It's a good idea to review the document each year to make sure it's still serving your company's needs.

The great thing about creating and enforcing a well-thought-out set of behavior standards is that over time your culture grows around it organically. Eventually, people won't be following the standards because a document tells them to, but because it feels right and natural to them. That's when you truly become a great place to work and a great company to do business with.

SAMPLE STANDARDS OF BEHAVIOR

Commitment to Coworkers

I recognize that my coworkers and I have a common destiny. What's good for them is good for me (and vice versa). In everything I say and do I will keep this truth in mind. Therefore . . .

I will strive to be helpful, and assist coworkers whenever possible. This includes coworkers in other departments.

I will always treat coworkers with respect. If I would consider it disrespectful if said to me, I won't say it to them, either.

I will welcome feedback from team members. Rather than being defensive, I will say thank you.

I will be respectful when approaching coworkers with criticisms, and offer them in private rather than public settings.

I will be mindful of coworkers' deadlines. I will respond promptly when they reach out with questions, comments, or concerns.

I will respect their time. I won't disrupt their schedules with meetings that run long or show up late to meetings.

If at all possible I will come to work on time. If I see I'm going to be late I will let people know ahead of time.

When I am absent, others have to pick up my slack. Therefore, I won't miss work unless I absolutely have to.

I will take ownership of projects. When problems come up I will do my best to solve them (regardless of where they come from).

I will strive to resolve issues with coworkers one on one if possible.

I won't talk about people or gossip behind their backs.

I will show respect for others' backgrounds and beliefs, even when they differ from my own.

When I take time off, I will set my coworkers up for success by letting them know what is going on so that work can continue seamlessly.

I will meet my deadlines. I will complete my assignments.

I will welcome new team members, mentor them when possible, and do everything in my power to help them succeed.

Creating a Positive Workplace

I will say, "Good morning" and greet people when I arrive at work. I will say, "Goodbye" when I leave to go home.

I will keep my office clean. I will also respect community spaces and clean up after myself.

I will strive to say three positive statements for every one negative.

I will avoid discussing controversial political or religious topics.

I will talk quietly when I am on the phone (or shut my door).

I will use good manners. This includes saying "please," "thank you," and "excuse me" when the occasion calls for it. It also includes knocking on doors.

Technology Etiquette

I will use my phone and computer for work purposes only.

I will not check social media accounts or make posts during work hours.

Even on my private accounts I will never post negative statements or sensitive information about my company, coworkers, clients, or customers.

I will use tools that make things easier on people, such as setting an away message on my email.

I will practice good email etiquette. For example:

- I will include a clear and direct subject line.
- I will avoid overwhelming people by copying them on unnecessary emails.
- I will craft emails carefully: I will include all relevant details but keep messages as short and to the point as possible.

I will be aware of potential computer viruses. I will open email from outside the facility only if I know the sender.

If at all possible I will not bring my cell phone to meetings. If I do I will check messages only during breaks.

Commitment to Clients

As often as possible I will put the client's needs ahead of my own. I will never forget that they are why we are in business and why my coworkers and I have jobs. Therefore . . .

I will do the best possible work I can to meet their needs.

I will be mindful of clients' privacy, and keep their information confidential.

I will be polite and open when speaking, and be aware of my body language during interactions.

I will acknowledge and maintain eye contact when interacting with them.

I will always treat clients in a professional and respectful way.

I will not complain about or say negative things about clients to my coworkers.

I will avoid discussing internal issues in public, or in the presence of clients.

I will check in regularly with clients to see if their expectations are met.

I will always be positive, upbeat, and courteous when interacting with clients.

I will never be frustrated when customers interrupt my day, remembering that meeting their needs are why we are in business.

If I'm unable to meet a customer's needs on my own, I will find a teammate who is able to do so.

When handing over clients, I will introduce colleagues and reassure the client that they will provide excellent service.

When I know a customer is dissatisfied, I will be proactive in correcting the situation.

I will strive for excellence in service recovery by using LEAP:
  L: Listen
  E: Empathize
  A: Apologize ("I'm sorry we did not meet your expectations.")
  P: Perform whatever action is necessary to correct the situation

Communicating with Clients and Customers

When a client calls or visits I will always introduce myself, and let them know what my role is.

I will say, "May I ask who is calling?" and direct their call appropriately if I can't handle it myself.

I will respond as quickly as possible when a client reaches out with a question.

I will promptly return missed calls and emails. I will not let a client go without a response for longer than 24 hours, even if I have to ask a colleague to respond in my absence.

I will learn clients' names, and use them when communicating.

I will avoid unpleasant behaviors, such as chewing gum or eating while on the phone.

I will avoid slang or abbreviations in emails.

I will always circle back and check in with those waiting on my response, even if I am not yet able to resolve their initial inquiry.

I will always be courteous of the client's time. If I must place them on hold, or if I can't respond to their email in a prompt and helpful manner, I will say, "I am so sorry for the inconvenience."

I will make things easier on the client by giving them an introduction and specific contact information when transferring them to another person. Also, I will take time to explain the situation to my colleagues when handing the client off to them so that the client doesn't have to repeat themselves over and over.

I will make a personal, brief, and effective voice-mail message so clients know who they are contacting when I'm unable to answer the phone.

I will narrate to the client what my next steps are when finishing the conversation, whether that means looking for more information, resolving their concern, or simply passing on a message to a colleague.

I will avoid frustrating clients with automated recordings, and will make every effort to connect them with a real person as soon as possible.

I will try hard to be available to take calls and respond to emails during business hours.

I will say thank you after every client interaction.

By signing below, I indicate that I have been given a copy of these Behavior Standards, and that I will try to uphold these standards to the best of my ability.

Name: _____

Date: _____

One copy will be signed and filed with Human Resources. Second copy will stay with employee.

33

The Power of Metrics:

How Measuring the Important Things Helps Us Be the Best We Can Be

How often does your company measure the items that make up its performance? Many businesses, especially newer or smaller ones, would have to answer sporadically, rarely, or in some cases, never. Maybe we just assume we're doing okay because we keep getting new customers or keep making payroll. Or maybe we think measurement is something we will get around to doing eventually. Or we just aren't sure what and how to measure.

The challenge is that when we can't see ourselves objectively, we don't realize what needs to change. And we can all get better in some area. This almost always requires measurement.

In my first book, *Hardwiring Excellence*, I shared nine principles that when followed produce great results. The first is a commitment to excellence. The second (a very close second) is "measure the important things." Don't measure just to measure, but measure what is most important to help you, the team you lead, or your company or community to be the best it can be.

Years ago, when I worked for an organization, a man named Clay Sherman taught our leadership team to measure. We did a great job of measuring finance items. That's not unusual, of course, because dollars and cents are easy to measure. However, we were lacking in measuring customer service and quality as well as the most important capital we had: human capital. I learned from Clay that we can tell a company's values by what they measure.

Measurement is vital, for it makes us aware of what does and does not need attention, where we are getting better or worse, or where there are some real red flags. Having objective data creates clarity, which energizes people and gets them focused on improvement. (As mentioned elsewhere in this book, vagueness is frustrating and anxiety-producing.) It allows the company to hold employees accountable for meeting goals. And because we can see when we've made an improvement, it allows us to celebrate wins, which keeps momentum going and results in more (and often bigger) wins in the future.

Doctors measure to check our health. When we board a plane, someone measures weight and its distribution. Recently when I was traveling, the warning light on the car I was driving came on and showed that the tires needed air. In this case, measurement allowed me to act before I had an accident or had to deal with a flat tire in $-21°$ temperatures. This last example shows the value of a dashboard. Businesses need dashboards, too—showing Key Performance Indicators (KPIs) and other crucial data—so they can identify issues as early as possible and know how to move forward.

In working with businesses, I have seen that once objective goals are set, it uncovers a need for better measurement. For example, when companies face the issue of attracting talent, they discover they have barriers in the recruitment process they were not aware of. How quickly are candidates responded to, reference checks done, interviews completed, and an offer made? We are in stiff competition for people, so it's urgent to communicate quickly to a candidate. The same is true of customer service. What are the standards for responding to a request or complaint? Each delay is costly to a company. In both cases, leaders need to be willing to measure. So why isn't measurement done nearly as well as it could be?

Since my latest book, *Building a Vibrant Community*, came out, I have been fortunate to speak with many community leaders, as well as be a guest on many radio shows and podcasts. And what I consistently find is that self-assessment is not easy. In a 12-step recovery program, Step 4 is "Made a searching and fearless moral inventory of ourselves." And it does not stop there. Step 5 asks us to share the inventory with another human being. There is a reason for this. Self-inventories, and authenticity in admitting what we need to do better, are crucial.

One challenge I see in my work with companies is that ego keeps us from holding up the mirror. A desire to say, "We are the best," might prevent a company from measuring. They are concerned that others may find out that it's not true. Recently a large company met with me to pitch their services. In the presentation they said, "We have the best service in the industry." When they were done, I asked how they knew they had the best service. They could not answer. Like a company telling an applicant, "We are a great place to work," if there has been no measurement around engagement, how can they back up their statement?

Now, in getting to know communities, I find that some can be even less comfortable with measurement. Every city says, "We have a great quality of life." But do they? One of the first items we recommend a city do is create a dashboard of key metrics and conduct a quality-of-life survey. The good news is that healthy communities quickly see the value of this.

Without good measurement, a person, a company, or a community can con themselves—what's often called "reading one's own press clippings." The key measurement we look at is population growth. Communities that are going in the right direction will have more people staying and more people moving in. It is not unusual to hear those in economic development tout the thousands of jobs and dollars they have brought into the county. Yet, they often have not had much positive population growth. To attract and retain jobs is good; however, if you don't gain more people living in the area, it does not have the impact it should have.

Leaders and companies that have the willingness and ability to do a searching and fearless moral inventory of themselves are those that will thrive. A few tips:

Take time to decide what is most important to you as a business. Companies in different industries will measure different things. In addition to customer satisfaction and employee engagement (covered in Chapter 19), a business might consider measuring cash flow, sales revenue, sales growth, customer acquisition cost, customer retention, net promoter score, lead-to-client conversion rates, market share, website visits, workforce turnover, product quality, and more. There are many great articles written on the subject of KPIs and I suggest every business owner research and study what's appropriate for their industry.

Don't try to measure too much at once. This will overwhelm people. Select a few KPIs to focus on first. You can set goals around these and focus on meeting them. Once you improve those you can move on to others.

If an accepted measurement tool exists, and many do, use it. Be careful not to rationalize how your company is different and thus the measurements don't apply. This is called "terminal uniqueness," and it will prevent you from improving and growing.

If a tool is not readily available, do your own survey. Years ago, a local high school had some very vocal parents who were not happy with the coach of a team. They were making a lot of noise. The coach came to see me. I offered to do a survey of the parents. The results showed that overall the parents were satisfied and that there also were some opportunities to improve. I rolled out the survey to the parents. The loud ones realized many other parents felt better about the coach than they had thought. The results also identified a road map for improvement for the coach.

If you're having trouble measuring something, look around. Ask others in your industry. Someone else has probably already done this. Avoid reinventing the wheel whenever you can.

Don't fight the data. Spend your time acting to improve the results. This might involve investing more resources in a key area, adding new employees, changing the way you hire, changing your marketing mix, focusing on a niche, etc.

Keep your results on a dashboard so you can see key metrics at all times. This will help you identify trends in "real time" so you can make quick decisions. You may also be able to make connections between seemingly unrelated data points.

Share performance metrics freely. It's best to have no secrets in a company (or at least as few as possible). Employees need to know how the company is doing in relevant areas so they can work to improve the numbers and feel good about progress made. Transparency creates ownership, which goes hand in hand with engagement.

Measure often enough to see if progress is being made. Once you see movement in a positive direction you can use it to reinforce the right behaviors in people.

Compare your metrics to your competition. It can be helpful to know how you stack up against others in your industry or marketplace.

Don't use the excuse that there is no comparison data. Even comparing your progress against yourself is worthwhile.

Yes, it can be hard to hold up the mirror. It takes time, effort, and energy, and issues like ego and fear can get in the way. However, getting better and better starts with a commitment to excellence and continues with the measurement of the most important things. We all need to have a clear picture of where we stand if we are to become the best we can be. It's true of individuals and communities and it is definitely true of businesses.

34

The Middle Manager Impact:

Why a Strong Leader Development System Is Crucial

A recent article in the *Wall Street Journal* suggested there could be a single fix for many of the big problems that companies experience: hiring better middle managers.[1]

The article featured a Gallup study from a few years back that found a company's productivity depends on the quality of these crucial leaders. The study found that managers didn't just influence the results of their teams, they explained a full 70 percent of the variance—something Gallup called "the single most profound, distinct and clarifying finding" in their 80-year history.

This didn't surprise me and I was really glad to see the role of the manager being recognized. I see this truth play out with many of the organizations I work with. Great middle managers are the key to creating great companies.

The irony is that middle managers often have the smallest training budget of any group in the organization. Given their level of responsibility, and their impact on organizational performance, this makes no sense.

Being a manager is hard. Good managers have to know dozens of skills. Plus, they face pressure from many directions: bosses, employees, and customers.

It's important that we hire and promote the right people for these critical positions and that we train them well. But first we need to understand exactly how managers impact an organization.

Here are just a few of the reasons middle managers are so important:

They are in a position to impact the greatest number of people and processes. Their actions can make or break a company. They typically supervise the greatest number of employees, are often closest to the products, the customers, and the vendors. Day-to-day operations are highly dependent on the leadership of middle managers.

Managers control the culture of the company. They must model values for everyone else and make sure others live up to them as well. They propel values forward.

They are on the front line with employees. As such, they are the key to employee engagement. They know what's going on. They know where the performance problems are and they know who's doing well.

They have a huge impact on attracting and retaining talent. Relationships matter in business, and nowhere do they matter more than between a middle manager and a direct report. Managers often determine how employees feel about their jobs. People don't quit the company; they quit their boss.

They're responsible for bringing out the best in people. They must be able to inspire and nurture creativity, innovation, teamwork, and so forth—the "soft skills" that are so important in today's complex business environment.

They're on the front line with daily processes. They know how things can be improved. They must manage a multitude of tasks and projects and make sure they get done efficiently.

They're the "messaging valve." They determine what gets reported to senior management and how news is broken to their direct reports.

They make change happen. People are never comfortable with change. It's up to managers to understand the psychology of change and move people through the various stages.

In short, managers have a hugely important and difficult job. We owe it to them (and to the organization!) to make sure they receive the resources and training they need to do it well. Please take a hard look at how well your company develops its middle managers—or, if you *are* a manager, what you can do to make sure you get the training you need.

All that said, it's vitally important for a business to know (a) what skills the leaders in your organization must have, and (b) how effective each one is in these areas. This can be achieved through a combination of self-assessment and assessment by a direct supervisor.

Tips for Developing Your Middle Management Team

For each manager in the organization, write down the top four measurable goals. One example for a sales manager may be to renew 90 percent of current clients. These goals usually fall into categories of revenue, expense management (productivity), employee engagement (turnover), or customer service.

Create a list of the skills necessary for a manager to meet the company's performance. This book contains many of the ones I feel are important. Your list may include others as well.

As an executive team, review the list of management skills. Decide which ones are best to focus on and train managers in. You will gain better consistency this way.

Have each manager rate their own proficiency for each skill on a 10-point scale. Every manager needs to be self-aware and coachable. This is a good exercise to help them start zeroing in on where they may need improvement.

Next, senior leaders should rate each manager who reports to them on a scale of 1–10 in each category. Hopefully, senior leaders and managers will agree on these ratings, but if not they can work together to do a deeper dive into the areas where there was disagreement.

Have each senior leader meet with their direct reports to create a development plan for each person. (The CEO will meet with each senior team member.) Certain skills are just more important for certain managers to master. It's necessary to prioritize to ensure that managers get the *right* training and development.

Senior leaders, ask each person: "What do you need from me to assist in your development?" "What barriers or challenges can I help with?" "Is there anything you feel will keep you from building your skill set to the point that you and the company's goals are reached?"

There are various ways you can provide this training. A leadership expert or coach for more formal training in a specific area can be brought in. Managers can attend off-site workshops or seminars. Managers can be matched with a mentor who is skilled in the needed area.

Often, there are local experts who can help. Use them to do training when you can. In Pensacola we are committed to helping local entrepreneurs and small business owners develop key leadership skills. We firmly believe that a thriving small business presence is the heart and soul of every vibrant community. (Helping new ventures get off the ground is important, but it's just as critical to help them master the skills they'll need to thrive—otherwise they may not be in business for long.)

That's why a series of monthly leadership development workshops featuring local experts are provided, as well as small business "roundtables" where owners can get together with a facilitator and talk about the issues they're facing. It's also why we host the annual business conference EntreCon®—it's a cost-effective, convenient way for local companies to get world-class training without the expense of travel. Visit www.studeri.org to learn more.

The organization with the best middle managers wins. Great leaders are great developers of people. This is both a responsibility and an honor—and few things are more rewarding than helping others become the best they can be.

Note

1. Sam Walker, "The Economy's Last Best Hope: Superstar Middle Managers," *Wall Street Journal*, March 24, 2019, https://www.wsj.com/articles/the-economys-last-best-hope-superstar-middle-managers-11553313606.

35

Hiring the Right People:

Creative Ways to Recruit and Hire

When talent is in short supply it's tough to find great job candidates that are right for your company. Even in slower economic times, when lots of people are looking for work, it's certainly not easy. That's why companies benefit from having a proven system in place for recruiting, hiring, and interviewing talent—one that gets good results wherever we are in the economic cycle. Without it, you're more likely to hire the wrong person.

Small companies in particular can make this mistake. They often hire quickly because they're overwhelmed and feel it's crucial to get a body in place. Yet when someone is hired and they don't work out, everyone loses: the organization, the manager, employees, customers, and vendors. Turnover is expensive, frustrating, and bad for morale. Sometimes it can take minutes to hire and years to fire—and having the wrong person on board can drive high performers away, discourage top talent from wanting to work for you, alienate customers, and hurt your business in countless other ways.

I've been fortunate to be able to speak with many leaders over the years about good hiring practices. Here are a few of my favorite strategies:

Create an internal team of recruiters. Instead of treating recruitment as a separate function, treat these people as business partners. People inside your company know better than anyone else the skills and behavior needed.

Ask around (and keep recruitment on your daily calendar). Tell people you're looking for a good employee and be specific about what you're looking for. You'll find people really want to help, and they'll often put some thought into it. Make a point to talk to everyone: vendors, clients, friends, etc. Invest a few minutes every day so the issue doesn't fall off the radar.

Let employees know you're looking for someone. They can be a great source of referrals. When I worked with companies, I recommended they meet with new employees after 30 days and again 60 days after their hire date to re-recruit them. One of the questions I had them ask is if they knew anyone from their old job who would be a valuable addition to the team. By then, they can tell others what it's like to work there!

Don't recruit just when you need someone. Build up a bench of potential talent. Interview likely candidates even if there is no job available yet. Then when you are ready to hire, it will be easy to make a great selection.

Partner with other business owners to exchange/refer talent. You can't hire everyone who comes your way, but you can send them to other companies. They will appreciate it and they will return the favor.

Keep your eyes open for great workers even in unexpected places. A friend of mine was shopping, and the salesperson was terrific (personable, service-oriented, etc.). She asked the salesperson if she had ever considered working in PR. She told her she would be great at it and would not have to work evenings and weekends. The salesperson jumped at the chance and quickly became an account manager at the agency.

Develop your leadership bench. Look at the talent you have and what you think you might need later and train with that in mind. Employees promoted internally have a significantly lower failure rate than do external hires.

Cross-train when you can. This gives you more flexibility, as some positions may be easier to fill than others. Employees may be willing to move around to other jobs inside the company to help fill empty positions.

A Few Things Not to Do

Don't rush to hire people. Be careful not to hire people who aren't really a good fit for your culture or don't really have the right skill set. Make sure your selection process achieves what you are trying to create. If you use focus groups, mix them up so they don't all look the same.

People tend to hire people who are most like them. While you want a culture fit, you don't want everyone to look the same.

Don't overpay to get someone. Be fair and competitive, but if you overpay, you will eventually become resentful. Plus, they might leave to join the next highest bidder.

Don't forget about retention. Don't focus so hard on attracting talent that you take your eye off retaining the talent you already have. Treat them well and keep them engaged. They may be getting pursued by other companies. Take good care of them! (See Chapter 36 for some ideas on retention.)

Probably the most important thing you can do to attract good people is to make sure your company is a great place to work. If there are glaring problems in your organization, make it a priority to fix them. When people are engaged, challenged, and given meaningful jobs to do, the best candidates will choose you out of all the possibilities in a tight job market (and your current employees will stick with you)!

The Interview Process: Peer Interviewing and Behavioral-Based Questions

Selection of talent is an area I have struggled with at times. I fall into the trap of liking a certain characteristic of an applicant enough that I miss red flags. For example, I've hired someone with great passion but missed the fact that they didn't have the other strong skills to do the job. One time years ago, after an extremely bad hire situation by me, which was painful for both sides, I surrendered and found help. I needed to learn how to hire better.

One of the most valuable tools I've discovered is peer interviewing. Basically, a company engages coworkers to work closely with the new hire in the interview process. Peer interviewing makes it more likely that the right candidate will be hired, and it also helps existing employees feel invested in that person's success.

In bigger companies, the sequence is that the Human Resource people screen and pass along to the manager who they feel would be a potential hire. The manager then interviews the applicants. They then send those they feel would be a good fit to the chosen peers. The leader does share what they think with the peer interviewers. The peers then interview the applicants and decide who should be hired.

Interviewers ask behavior-based questions based on objective criteria (more on this below) and assess the candidate on their answers. They also pay attention to personality and temperament. Later, each member of the team can make a recommendation on who to hire, though the leader has the final say. (However, in most cases it's a good idea to choose the person recommended by the peer interview team.)

Now, on to behavioral-based interviewing. Essentially, this means you ask questions that reveal how an applicant has handled situations in the past related to teamwork, customer service, problem solving, time management, communication, and motivation/values. Behavior-based questions can give us a more in-depth glimpse into a skill set that's hard to glean from a resume and cover letter.

Here's an example for each category:

Teamwork: *Provide me with a time when you struggled while working on a team. How did you handle that?*

Customer Service: *Share a time when you made sure a customer was satisfied with the service.*

Problem Solving: *Tell me about a time when you were under a lot of pressure at work. What was taking place and how did you get through it?*

Time Management: *Give me an example of a time when you had to complete numerous tasks. How did you handle that?*

Communication: *Tell me about a time you had to explain something so someone at work would understand it better.*

Motivation and Values: *Describe a situation when you saw a problem and took time to correct it rather than waiting to hear from another person to do so.*

What to Look for in the Candidates You Interview

"What do you look for in an employee?" It's a question often asked to company executives. In fact, there is a profile on a successful business person in the *New York Times* each Sunday, and somewhere in the interview that question is always included.

While it may seem like an easy question, the answer isn't always straightforward. It depends on various factors. What's the role you're hiring for? What is the skill set of your current workforce? How is the company performing? Those can all dictate the kind of employee you are looking for at any given time.

Here are some of my thoughts: role plays a key part in what to look for in an employee. When selling a product at a retail store, the employee needs to focus on the customer they're dealing with but also keep an eye on other customers in the store, so they don't lose them. However, at the counter, getting the items priced and rung up accurately takes a single focus.

Balancing out the skill set of a company is also important. Sometimes an ideal employee comes along, but may not be the right fit at the time based on who else is already in the department. Years ago, I applied for a new role within my organization and did not get it. The reason? At the time they needed someone with stronger technical skills. I was too much like what they already had in the department.

Finally, it depends on the organization's performance. Let's say sales are below expectations and a sales clerk job is open. Because of performance, someone with a proven track record is a requirement due to a lack of time to train a less experienced employee. If sales are above target, you might be more willing to hire a person with perhaps a bigger "upside" who will need more training. Often, whether you hire someone or not comes down to timing.

So, what am I looking for when I make hires? Here are five key factors:

1. **Are they passionate?** This does not mean the person has to be an extrovert. But in their own way, it needs to be obvious that they are relentless about doing a good job.
2. **Are they proactive?** This one is high on my list. I'm looking for someone who is willing to take action before being asked. Years ago, I'd have a subtle test for this when I was handling interviews. I would put a crumpled-up piece of paper in the hallway on the way to my office. The location would be very obvious, somewhere front and center where the interviewee couldn't miss it. As they came down the hallway, I would notice whether they picked up the piece of paper and threw it away or just walked by it. Guess who didn't get the job?

3. **Are they coachable?** Today's job will change. How coachable is the person? Prior to hiring there are excellent questions you can ask that helps decipher that. For example, you might ask them to tell you about a time when they doubted their ability to do a job. Hopefully, they will tell you that they asked for help or sought out some other means of skill development. After hiring I look for these things: if I forward an article to them to read, do they send me their response? If they do without asking it hits on point No. 2 (proactivity) and No. 3 (coachability). If I mention a book that will help, do they read it on their own? Are they looking for ways to improve themselves and the organization?

4. **Can they handle feedback?** While common for people to say they want feedback, in most cases I find that truly they mean only *positive* feedback. Yes, positive feedback is important, but to really improve a person must be able to receive and act on feedback that will not be positive. It is not meant to hurt but to help.

5. **Can they provide constructive feedback to me and others to make things better?** Everyone must be committed to pointing out what could be better. It seems that many times when a bad outcome is noticed, some people in the organization had concerns. However, when they diagnosed this problem initially, they did not want to step on toes. So, they stayed silent. In some cases, maybe they spoke up but were ignored by management. Toe steppers are welcomed. The more value-driven a person is, the more assertive they will be to speak up if there are issues.

There are far more key factors, but these five, in my opinion, are the ones that separate the good employees from the great ones. While you can't always tell in the interview whether a candidate has these qualities, you can usually get a good idea about at least some of them.

A company is only as good as its people. Every new hire either adds to or detracts from the culture you're trying to create. Don't leave employee selection to chance. Put a process in place and you'll greatly improve your odds of building a powerhouse team that consistently becomes more and more high-performing and successful in the future.

Retention:

36 *The First 90 Days and Beyond*

One of the biggest issues that keep business owners and leaders up at night is finding and hiring talent. Hiring people takes time. Not only does it require precious hours for leaders to go through applications and interviews to fill a position, it takes time to get a new employee fully acclimated to a job. Also, hiring people takes money. There's a cost to bringing in interviewees. It is expensive to put new people on payroll and benefits and to get them up to speed.

So yes, the acquisition of quality people is vital. But what may go unnoticed is the energy needed to get that person off to a great start.

Many business owners and leaders know the risk of losing an employee within the first year, but few may realize just how many employees leave before they've even hit *90 days*. The statistics range from 20 to 30 percent, and while I'm not sure of the exact number, I've seen firsthand in my work with organizations over the years that too many people leave their job before they've really even gotten started.

These early departures are both disappointing and costly. What happens when people leave? We've established that turnover costs a lot of time and money. But there's more. When people leave, the remaining employees will likely have to work additional hours. That can lead to burnout and stress on employees and family. And, ultimately, this will negatively impact the customer experience as well.

With a little bit of energy and focus on an employee's first 90 days, you can lay the groundwork for a productive and engaged employee. Getting really intentional about making sure new hires are getting the things they need and helping relieve anxiety can make a huge difference. (Starting a new job is stressful!) It's not only a chance to impress the employee, but it's likely old coworkers, friends, and family will be asking how they like their new job. This gives them a chance to say positive things about your company (and possibly attract additional employees). You have a real opportunity to promote the brand of your company if you can get a few things right.

All of that said, here are some tips to help get new employees off to a roaring start:

Don't oversell the new hire. This is a common mistake. A leader hires someone they feel will be a "superstar" and overhypes them. This does *not* set the new hire up for success. It shines a spotlight on them and creates a lot of pressure. If they turn out not to be right for the job after all, you might be reluctant to let them go because you don't want to admit you made a mistake. Existing employees aren't eager to help the new hire because they resent what a big deal you made about them. Meanwhile, the person knows they aren't measuring up, which is a painful spot to be in. Don't go overboard announcing a new hire. (Always put the focus on the team, not the new person.) Make sure they're open to learning. Be judicious and restrained in praising them. And, of course, if you realize you've made a bad hire, it's far better to admit the mistake early on.

Don't rush the new employee into action. Employees do better if they learn about their employer before they jump into their job. Take time to orient the employee to the history of the organization: why the organization exists, including the mission, vision, and values of the company. Review the standards of behavior and the safety rules. Make sure they understand the roles of people they will be working with, where to go with questions, and what they should expect in the first 90 days. If the employee will be representing a product to customers, take the time to make sure the employee knows the product inside and out.

Assign a buddy to train the new person. Pick out a peer to help train the new hire. I have seen these people called a buddy, a preceptor, or a mentor. Whatever you call this person, choose them carefully. Many times, buddies are not prepared for this role. They need to understand the basics of staff development. A new employee naturally tends to compare themselves to the person training them. If that person isn't empathetic to being a newbie—explaining it took them time to learn everything they know, for example—the new employee often gets scared. They think they may not make it so they quit. This is a big reason for early departures.

Make it worth the trainer's time. While trainers want the new employee to be successful, it's important to provide some compensation for filling this important role. It doesn't need to be a huge amount. Pay half of this during the training and withhold half. The other half gets paid out at an agreed upon time (one year is the norm but it varies) if the new employee this person trained is still at the organization and is meeting expectations. This will encourage them to stay engaged.

Check in often. This doesn't just mean the usual "How are you doing?" Be specific and intentional. Make sure they feel wanted, heard, recognized, and are comfortable. And after 90 days, survey the employee about the hiring and on-boarding process, asking about what works and what needs to get better.

Celebrate. Have an orientation or on-boarding graduation in which the employee receives a diploma and a small gift. The buddy should also be recognized.

Set the New Employee Up for Success by Showing What Success Looks Like ——————

Of course, new employees want to do a great job. That's why it's crucial to let them know exactly what "great" looks like. In Chapter 32 we talk about having job candidates sign a standard of behavior contract even before you interview them. In addition, once you hire a new person, you might consider sharing exactly what you think being a highly effective employee looks like in action. Here is my take on the habits that great employees cultivate:

Great employees know what the *what* is for their boss (and act on it). When an employee knows what matters most to the boss, they can laser-focus on meeting their needs in this area. Let's say they've noticed negativity drives their boss crazy. Once they realize this, they can make an effort to frame their communications with them in a positive way. (See Chapter 22.)

They know that the ball is always in their court. Once the boss gives an assignment, they do what they need to do to move it forward quickly. Great employees *never* let themselves be the hold-up. They check in with the boss regularly on the project so they don't have to bring it up.

When they're not sure, they ask *why*. Hopefully, leaders already explain the "why" behind what employees are being asked to do. But if this doesn't happen, great employees ask rather than assume the worst.

They go out of their way to be likeable and make people happy. When employees make a point to be friendly and helpful, they contribute to the "emotional bank account" at work. These deposits have a big impact—and they reduce the pain of the inevitable withdrawals. Coworkers will return the favor and forgive them when they make a mistake.

They resolve coworker issues one-on-one. Taking a conflict to the boss, who then must discuss it with their boss, who may then have to get an HR rep involved, is time-consuming and unproductive. Yes, there are times when they have to go through official channels and involve HR, but often an issue with a coworker can be solved with a face-to-face adult conversation.

They apologize when it's called for. All employees make mistakes. It's what they do afterward—after they've dropped the ball or missed a deadline or got caught in the act of gossiping about a coworker—that truly determines their character as employees and coworkers.

They do the little extra things that make customers happy. Often, it's the little things that keep people coming back to their favorite stores, restaurants, or other businesses. It's the server who knows exactly how they take their coffee or the plant nursery owner who calls to let them know a shipment of their favorite flowering shrubs just arrived. Great employees go the extra mile, without having to be asked (whether it's in their job description or not).

They see complaints as gifts. When complaints are handled well, customer loyalty will skyrocket. Great employees don't get defensive when customers complain. They know they're hearing valuable feedback that can help the organization improve its service. They listen, they sincerely apologize, and they take action to make things right.

They never blame, finger-point, or badmouth their company or coworkers. These habits are deeply destructive to the company's image. *Everyone* needs to be engaged in building the organization's brand. That means it's critical to "manage up" their company, its products, and their coworkers with every customer interaction—and when they're off the clock as well.

They appreciate the boss. Employees are often quick to point out what their boss got wrong or didn't do, but when's the last time they thanked their boss for a flexible schedule, training or personal development, or creating a positive work environment? It's easy to take these things for granted, but the praise and gratitude goes a long way.

While these qualities and behaviors may seem like common sense, this isn't always the case. Most of the time a new employee will appreciate having them spelled out. I find that clarity is always welcome; knowing what's expected of us always reduces anxiety and helps us make the kinds of decisions that allow us to thrive.

Keeping Your Great New Hires

Employees can usually tell early on what the culture of a company is like and it's these early impressions that help them decide whether to stay or go. Some may leave in the first 90 days and some may leave later, after they've had a chance to find and look for a new job. Focusing on retention is a 365-day-a-year job and on-boarding isn't a one-time process, but more of a continuous motion.

When a person quits it's usually not a sudden decision. The actual resignation can start weeks, months, and at times, years earlier. Every day is a day that the leader must focus on retention of employees. If they're not skilled in retention, they get lots of experience in recruitment.

In a very real way, creating a culture that attracts, engages, and retains the best employees is what this entire book is about. After all, it's great leaders who create great cultures. So it's challenging to single out specific practices that impact retention—because everything is intertwined and it all works together. However, I do want to hit a few high spots that I feel positively impact retention:

Measure employee engagement and always be working to improve it. There's a reason this subject is mentioned several times in this book. It's so important to know how engaged employees are (as discussed in Chapter 19) and to make sure you are working to capture their hearts and minds. Engaged employees are much less likely to leave.

Make sure you (and all leaders) are well trained so they can give employees what they want and need. Most people don't leave their job, they leave their boss. This is why it's important that all leaders inside their organization are able to make sure employees can answer the following questions with a confident yes:

- Do I know what's expected from me at work?
- Do I have the material and equipment I need to do my work right?
- At work, do I have the opportunity to do what I do best every day?
- In the past seven days have I received recognition or praise for doing good work?
- Does someone at work seem to care about me as a person?
- Is there someone at work who encourages my development?

Show those you supervise that you care for them beyond the workplace. This is preventive retention. Consistently ask questions beyond just "how are you?" A tip I learned years ago from a supervisor is to send birthday cards to your employees' children. I have done this for years. What does it accomplish? First, I know the names and ages of the children. I know when their birthdays are so when I see the employee I can say something. It is usually the first time this has happened to an employee. I receive nice notes from the children and it is a deposit in the retention "bucket." Of course, we also send birthday cards to employees.

Don't wait to provide feedback and development conversations. It is all too common for a supervisor to have a development talk once a year. Surveys consistently show employees want development. Say to them, *We are committed to your development and want to invest in you. What skill would like to develop?* If the employee can't think of one, ask them to take their time and in the next few weeks you want to meet with them to hear their thoughts. If they are still unsure, bring up your ideas. This again shows caring via the investment in the person. It's shown over and over again that Millennials in particular put a very high premium on development.

Ask, "Is there any reason you would leave here?" On a regular basis include this with such questions as "Whom should I recognize?" and "Do you have the tools necessary to do your job?" Don't be afraid of this question. It leads to great conversation.

Trust the employees and solicit their input. Employee engagement surveys show it is not unusual to see issues listed like communication and teamwork. This is even more likely if some employees are working virtually. Throw this back to the employees. Ask a group or all the employees how they think communication can get better. Same with teamwork. Employees want to be included and their input valued.

How new employees experience those first 90 days is deeply important. You want them to immediately feel at home and excited about the company they have joined. And smart owners and leaders know that those three months or so are just the beginning. There is nothing more important than creating an organizational culture that engages, challenges, and even delights employees. When employees are happy, customers are happy. And when customers are happy, the company thrives.

37 Create a Training and Development System That Motivates Employees to Learn

The business world is changing fast. With rapid advances in technology and shifting consumer behavior, lots of jobs are being created that didn't exist 10 years ago. A recent PBS article cited an Institute for the Future study predicting that "eighty-five percent of the jobs that today's students will do in 2030 don't exist yet."[1]

Now, this particular article focused on what colleges are doing to adapt to a quickly changing workplace, but it made me think about what this means for employers. It's no longer just a matter of having to train new graduates so they'll be work ready; even seasoned employees are now in a position where they must constantly learn new skills. Moving forward, employers will have to play an increasingly vital role in training and developing their workforce.

We've known for a long time that when it's done well, training highly benefits companies and employees alike. For one thing, it helps organizations create the kind of culture that attracts and retains great talent, which is especially important when the economy is booming and good candidates are scarce. It also helps organizations keep up with industry changes, stay ahead of competitors, get employees engaged and motivated, and more.

And, of course, it's good for the employees themselves. It helps them get better and better at what they do and advance in their company and career.

So yes, having a solid development system in place is more crucial than it has ever been. But it's one thing to offer training to your employees. It's another thing for employees to embrace it. Too often, they don't take advantage of learning and development resources already available.

Most leaders know that employees can be cynical about development. Sometimes they feel they're too busy to take time off work for training. Other times, they believe (for various reasons) that the training they've had in the past wasn't effective or meaningful.

We need to be able to teach in a way that makes employees want to learn. It's no longer enough just to get people "up to speed" when we hire them. Development is an ongoing part of the job, and employees need to accept and welcome that reality. The more eager they are to learn, the more successful the development efforts will be.

The good news is that most people really do care about professional development. For example, a recent Gallup survey found that 87 percent of Millennials said professional or career growth and development are extremely important to them.

And it's not *just* Millennials. In Pensacola, we at Studer Community Institute find that our monthly leadership development workshops and small business roundtables are incredibly well received and well attended by professionals of all ages.

Our workshop series is focused on helping entrepreneurs and small business leaders master foundational skills like hiring, firing, employee engagement, creating revenue streams, process improvement, marketing, and so forth.

We also offer small business roundtables in which owners get together with a facilitator and talk about the problems they're facing. These sessions are done in small groups (generally four to eight people) and are led by a good facilitator. Like the workshops, the roundtables are about training and development but are more intense and focused.

The success of our workshops and roundtables shows that people truly are motivated to learn—*when they believe that the training is valuable to them.* We are fortunate to be able to offer the kind of training people value and find the right experts to lead it.

Your company can do the same. When you get your training and development right, you'll build a culture that attracts the best and brightest and build the kind of foundation that makes you a high-performing organization.

Here are a few tips:

Supervisors should see themselves as chief development officers. Think about your own work experiences. Who played a key part in your own development? It was most likely your supervisor. This is why strong leader development is a vital investment for a company. The more skilled the supervisor, the better they will be at helping others develop to the best of their abilities. This includes understanding the psychology of change and growth and how best to lead people through those times when it gets difficult.

Make sure everyone understands that learning a new skill causes discomfort. When we ask employees (or anyone) to learn a new skill we are asking them to move through several psychological states: from being comfortable to being unsettled and, eventually, to a state of *unconscious competence* where they can almost practice the new skill in their sleep. Here I am referring to a theory that was developed at Gordon Training International by employee Noel Burch in the 1970s. The four stages of competence are:

1. **Unconscious incompetence.** The person does not know what they don't know.
2. **Conscious incompetence.** The individual recognizes their shortcomings and the value of learning the skill. (This is where they feel the most discomfort.)
3. **Conscious competence.** The person now knows the steps needed for success; however, they are still in that learning phase.
4. **Unconscious competence.** The behavior is now so embedded in the person it becomes second nature. This leads to the ability to multitask. The behavior is so ingrained that the skill is performed even while doing another task.

To manage any kind of change, including the learning of new skills, supervisors need to understand these phases. It's the only way to help employees move through that "unsettled feeling" and do and say the right things to keep them on track and forging ahead.

Keep training as close as possible to the job people really do every day. One reason our Pensacola workshops are so successful is that we think hard about relevancy. For example, if a business has only three employees, hiring is probably not the most important thing in the world to them—but creating revenue streams is. When people can clearly see how training makes their lives easier, they'll want to learn.

Connect to the *why*. People always want to know what's in it for them. Why do they need to learn this new skill? How will it benefit them personally? How will it make their work more meaningful? How will it benefit the company? Share this information as many times and in as many different ways as it takes until they see the value. This will help them keep going as they travel through the difficult process of learning something new.

Train across many areas. Functional skills matter, but don't neglect leadership and relationship-building skills. "Soft" skills and emotional intelligence are more crucial than they've ever been. In a world where Artificial Intelligence is taking over many of the jobs humans used to do, people at all levels need to be good at collaborating, communicating, and innovating—things computers can't do.

Be as flexible as you can. Everyone is different, and therefore we all learn differently. Not everyone absorbs and processes information the same way. Some people need lots of one-on-one coaching while others are more self-sufficient. Some do fine in a classroom setting, while others like online learning they can complete on their own time.

Of course, it's not always possible to tailor each person's learning to their individual preferences, but do it when you can. In general, try not to rely too heavily on online courses as not everyone is wired to learn well that way. Consider lecture formats, books, online videos, hands-on training with feedback, and other methods.

Practice what you preach. As often as possible, take the training with employees. This sends the signal that what they're learning matters to you and the company.

Encourage more-skilled employees to help with training. Most people love sharing their knowledge and experience. And other employees will appreciate learning from peers—it helps them see the relevancy of what they're hearing.

Don't just tell them. Show them. Theory and instruction are great, but people learn best when they see a skill in action or—even better—have a chance to practice it right away. Role-playing "labs" can be really effective, especially when training in leadership skills. In general, make training as interactive as possible. This will help the concept "stick."

Don't overwhelm people. Train on one skill at a time and break training up into manageable chunks. Long, intensive training sessions crammed full of content just don't work. People can't process that much information at once. Keep training sessions as short and focused as you can, and people are more likely to retain and practice what they've learned. This also ensures they'll be able to get their "real" work done.

Set goals and give employees regular feedback on how they're applying what they're learning. This shows them that the training is meaningful to the company. And when they know they're being "graded" and held accountable, they'll take what they're learning more seriously. They'll see it as part of their job, not something that takes them away from it.

Hold progress meetings with employees (not just annual reviews) and ask about training and development. I have found that employees do best when they get regular feedback from their supervisor. One solution that seems to work well is to hold quarterly reviews with each employee. While these meetings cover a lot of territory (see Chapter 38), they should definitely include questions about training and development. You can ask employees how they feel about the training they've received, what skills they'd like to master in the near future, and so forth.

Reward and recognize progress. The whole idea is for people to improve, so when you see someone making progress, praise that person. Publicly recognize them. This encourages more of the same.

As the business world gets more complex, we must all get better and better at learning. The better your company is at training and developing—and the more enthusiastic your employees are about learning new skills—the more prosperous your company will be. Make it a priority, invest some time and thought into it, and do everything you can to get people on board. Your efforts will pay off for years to come.

Note

1. Gretchen Frazee, "How Colleges Are Preparing Students for Jobs That Don't Exist Yet," *Making Sen$e*, PBS NewsHour, December 6, 2018, https://www.pbs.org/newshour/economy/making-sense/how-colleges-are-preparing-students-for-jobs-that-dont-exist-yet.

38 Performance Reviews That Make a Difference

Do you dread annual performance reviews? Many people—both leaders and employers—feel this way, for a variety of reasons.

Leaders may dislike performance reviews because they're not clear on how to evaluate employees. They may not have a good set of criteria to grade them by so the entire process is marked by ambiguity and vagueness. Like most people, they may hate giving negative feedback. In general they end up feeling like performance reviews are an expensive waste of (already very scarce) time—since each year they go through the process and nothing ever changes.

Employees dread performance reviews as well. They may go into these meetings with no idea what they're about to hear because they've received little feedback along the way. However, human nature being what it is, they are probably fearing the worst. During the review itself they sit there feeling judged and criticized and they may leave feeling not too positive toward their leader. Employees want to see their leaders as supporters and allies but a traditional performance review can make them seem like adversaries.

The scenario I've just described is obviously bad for all parties concerned. Rather than motivating employees, it can create fear, resentment, and other negative feelings. It's not surprising there's been a big push in recent years to get rid of the annual performance review altogether. Yet most companies continue to hold them.

The great news is that performance reviews don't have to be like this. I've worked with many companies that have figured out how to do them in a way that gets great results.

The fact is, a well-designed and well-executed performance evaluation system—based on clear goals and objective metrics and held in conjunction with ongoing, all-year-long feedback—can have amazing benefits for your company. Here are just a few examples:

- It shows you who is doing well and who isn't. It helps you identify who deserves pay increases and promotions.
- It may also help you identify where more training is needed. If a performance review shows that an employee is struggling in a particular area it might not be a will issue but a skill issue. Especially if it is a trend across several people's reviews, you'll know to strengthen training in that area.
- It keeps the team aligned. It keeps people focused on and working toward company goals.
- It's fair. Employees are scored on objective, quantifiable metrics: either they met the goal or they didn't. Leaders aren't tempted to judge employees on subjective qualities like charisma or likeability.
- It creates a culture of ownership and accountability. Employees know exactly what they're being graded on. This spurs them to "own" their area and solve problems because they are being rewarded on results, not efforts.
- It helps employee performance get better and better. This is good for organizational outcomes, of course, but it also keeps employees engaged and motivated. Most people want to improve and grow.
- It helps you move low performers up or out. If you're not careful these people can suck the life out of leaders. A good evaluation system frees you up to focus more on coaching high performers and do other high-level work. (Moving low performers out of the organization also makes your good employees happy!)
- It creates a culture that helps attract the best talent and retain them once they've been hired.

Here are some tips for putting in place a performance evaluation system that works:

Choose an evaluation tool that uses objective measures, not subjective ones. Many organizations evaluate employees using measures like *exceeds expectations, meets expectations, does not meet* expectations. But what do these words really mean? They mean whatever the leader doing the performance review interprets them to mean. But perceptions vary. What looks like "exceeds" to one leader may look like "meets" to others—or even "does not meet." Far better to evaluate employees on *objective* metrics, whether it's number of sales made, amount of revenue brought in, number of items produced, Net Promoter scores, or whatever makes sense for them. It's hard to argue with numbers!

Make sure reviews are based on clear, measurable, timely goals. People need to know exactly what they're being judged on. They also need to know the consequences if goals aren't met. This motivates people to perform and encourages accountability at every level. And when you have a system of continuous feedback in place (more on this later) people will know if they've met their goals or are at least on track to meet them. There will be no surprises during the annual performance review.

For leaders in particular you may also want to "weight" goals. If a leader has five goals they are being evaluated on but three of them are actually more important, you could weight them accordingly. The three more important goals might have weights of 30 percent each. The two less important ones could have weights of 20 percent. This makes it very clear which activities the leader should prioritize in order to get a positive performance review.

Connect individual goals to larger organizational goals. It's surprising how few companies structure performance reviews this way, but they should—it gets everyone aligned and working toward the same outcomes. It's especially important when evaluating leaders. I've seen organizations give most of their leaders a "substantially exceeds" rating, yet when I looked at the organization's yearly goals almost all of them were missed.

It's also a good idea to get employees involved in setting and shaping organizational goals and be transparent about progress toward them. When you do these things, employees are more likely to buy into the goals and be motivated to work toward them. Then during performance reviews employees will have a strong foundation for having a productive discussion around their role in having met (or not met) the organization's larger goals.

Don't just meet once a year. Meet (at least) four times a year. The "official" annual performance review should be the culmination of several smaller meetings that came before. This makes far more sense than ignoring performance throughout most of the year and then suddenly springing a "grade" on employees. A quarterly review system will force leaders to coach employees and keep track of their progress all year long (rather than noticing what they're doing right before the annual review).

This is a great relationship builder. It also makes reflection and striving for improvement and growth an ongoing part of the employees' work life rather than a once-a-year effort that quickly falls to the wayside when things get back to normal.

During all of these conversations, take a different approach for each level of performer. Most organizations have three types of employees: a small group of poor performers, a larger group of high performers, and a majority of employees that fall somewhere in the middle. During these quarterly conversations as well as the yearly one it's important to address each type differently. Specifically:

High performers: Praise them, thank them, and let them know you want to keep them. Share your goals for the company and ask if they have any suggestions. Ask what you can do to make their job or life better.

Mid-level performers: Tell them why you value them. Alleviate their anxiety by talking about their good qualities. Explain what they can do better (usually just one item so as not to overwhelm the employee) and enlist them in a conversation on what they can do to improve and develop.

Poor performers: Explain exactly how the employee is not meeting expectations. (It's important to have specifics documented so you can give them hard examples of what you mean, including dates and outcomes.) Then tell them exactly what needs to be done to improve, then spell out the consequences that will occur if they don't.

If a poorly performing employee does not improve over several quarterly reviews (at most) you will have a tough decision to make. Do not let them stick around too long. They will end up draining all your energy and taking up valuable time you should be spending in more positive ways. Plus, higher-performing employees will resent them. They may even leave.

Make it clear that performance reviews are a two-way street. You want employees to give feedback and input. Think conversation, not confrontation. You're not handing down a sentence, you're having a meaningful exchange that strengthens your relationship and leads to growth and improvement on both sides. Performance reviews should be thought of as a conversation between two adults. It should not feel like a parent scolding a child or a teacher reprimanding a misbehaving student.

Don't sugarcoat, but do make reviews more positive than negative. Especially with high- and mid-level performers, spend more time talking about strengths, positive achievements, and growth opportunities than negative aspects. Remember the 3-to-1 ratio! (See Chapter 18.) You want employees to feel positive about you and the organization because positivity is inherently connected to engagement and performance.

Get in the habit of giving on-the-spot feedback all year long. When someone has made a mistake it's better to tell them in the moment rather than waiting a year or even a quarter. The same is true of rewarding and recognizing and saying thank you. That's why the most effective leaders practice regular rounding (see Chapter 17)—it helps them see what's going on and respond appropriately right away. Giving frequent feedback sets a productive context for quarterly and yearly performance reviews. Many issues will have been raised and addressed earlier, leaving deeper, more meaningful subjects to be addressed during the reviews.

A great performance evaluation system can change the culture of your company in profound ways. How you motivate and reward people is everything. When they feel they are being treated fairly, that leaders care about their success and growth, and that they are working toward clear and meaningful goals, they *will* give their best effort.

As people improve and see the results of that improvement they will become more motivated and passionate. Soon you will see an ever-improving cycle of organizational performance. This is the kind of momentum that takes a company from *good* to *great* to *even greater*—not a bad payoff for rethinking a flawed system that no one liked in the first place.

39 Customer Satisfaction Starts with Employee Engagement:

Have a Process to Regularly Measure Both

Engaged employees create satisfied customers and vice versa. When employees feel their work has meaning and purpose, they are driven to go above and beyond to make customers' lives better. Then, when customers express that they are satisfied, employees become even more engaged. It's a virtuous cycle and it positively impacts every part of your business. This is why it's so important for a company to have a system in place to regularly measure both parts of the equation.

The effort from an engaged employee can take a business from average to great (and the absence of that effort can take it from below average to out of business). Engaged employees think and act like owners; they are emotionally committed to meeting organizational goals. They understand the impact they have on the company's success. They take care of equipment and supplies as if they were their own. They are deeply invested in the customer's happiness and success because they understand that these things are directly linked to their own future. All of this leads to better word of mouth, more customers, and better job security and wages.

Ultimately, employee engagement means better financial performance, greater customer satisfaction, higher quality, fewer absences and turnover, better safety, and easier talent recruitment. (See Chapter 19 for tips on creating engaged employees.)

My first experience with the link between employee engagement and customer satisfaction was back in the 1990s. I was the senior vice president of Holy Cross Hospital in Chicago and had been given the assignment to raise patient (customer) satisfaction. When I first received the assignment, I did what I thought would make the difference. After a few months, it was obvious as the measured results came in, my way was not working. If I could not achieve the results my boss expected, my career was not going to go well.

Out of desperation, I turned to Southwest Airlines. Midway Airport, which had an educational center in which employees learned the "Southwest way," was located nearby.

Keep in mind that this was all happening at a time when a big change was taking place. Customers were getting more vocal about what they wanted and needed. Their expectations were higher than before. Southwest Airlines' cofounder and CEO Herb Kelleher—who passed away during the writing of this book—was one of the first people to figure out that simply getting people from point A to point B was no longer enough. The experience itself mattered, too.

This echoed what was going on in healthcare. It was becoming obvious that clinical quality, which is where hospitals focus a lot of their time, was just expected and had become the price of entry. Now hospitals also had to get a lot of other things right as well, including the patient experience.

When I got to the airport, I introduced myself and explained my role at the hospital and the fact that we just could not move our customer satisfaction results. I also shared that this was because we were big, we had lots of government rules to follow, we were in a tough neighborhood, we were different from Southwest because we were in healthcare, and so on. Later I learned that I had fallen into the trap of terminal uniqueness—rationalizing how different one is as an excuse not to change.

The bottom line is that Southwest held up a mirror in which I saw myself more clearly. It started with their listening and then asking me questions. They asked me to go over with them what I was doing. I explained that I shared with the employees how important patient satisfaction is, that it is not rocket science, that these are things we learned in kindergarten, and to just treat people like they want to be treated. They asked me how that was working. I said it was not working well, and, in fact, our results had gotten worse rather than better.

In a very nice way, they said, "We think you have things in the wrong order." I asked, "What do you mean?" They replied that customer satisfaction starts with employee satisfaction. Then they asked me some questions. *How do the employees like working at Holy Cross Hospital? Do they feel they have a good supervisor? Do they have the tools, equipment, and systems they need to do a good job? Do they feel recognized for good performance? Do they receive training? How much training does management receive? How are you measuring employee satisfaction?*

Very quickly I had entered the arena of conscious incompetence, meaning I was suddenly recognizing my shortcomings. Even though I had somehow been promoted to a top leadership role, it was evident to me that I had much to learn. Keep in mind that prior to coming to Chicago, I had worked in public education and at the only hospital in the city where I lived. At the time, if you wanted to teach in the city or work in healthcare, you had only one choice. We also did not measure taxpayer satisfaction or employee satisfaction. We just assumed it was fine because some people stayed there a long time. In this case, I realized how wrong I had been!

My to-do list when I left that meeting was to measure employee satisfaction, find out what was working and why, identify areas for improvement, and create a development program in which all leaders could acquire the skills needed to be successful. I needed to create conditions where if a leader could not create a great place for the staff to work, they would not be able to stay. The Southwest people also said that this training must be mandatory and that all the other executives and I must be front and center at all sessions. They then offered to let us use their training facilities for these sessions so we could focus on these issues with fewer distractions.

This conversation and the actions taken afterward changed my life.

It was definitely a scary time. I was asked to do things like turn the organizational chart upside down. My job was to make sure everyone who led people had the skills to do so, and it started with me. Southwest shared that when I saw employees, I needed to make sure I asked them whether they had what they needed to do their job that day. In fact, it seemed to me that I was working for the employees rather than having them work for me. "Exactly!" the people at Southwest said. "You're starting to catch on."

I got to meet with Kevin and Jackie Freiberg while they were writing their book *Nuts! Southwest Airlines' Crazy Recipe for Business and Personal Success.* They even came to Holy Cross to see how we were doing. And it turned out that we did well once we put people first—starting with those closest to the customer.

Soon a magazine came to do a story on us. They interviewed several employees. They asked: *What is different? Not too long ago, Holy Cross was not doing well financially. You are still in the same area, and in same facility, so what has changed?* Tom Badell, a housekeeper, said, "They used to focus on money and lost it, and now they focus on people and we make it." Tom said it best.

We also learned that when you get the "people" part right, the other results will happen: better quality, better service, better efficiency, and, yes, much better financial results.

I learned so much in those years. For example, as mentioned earlier, I learned about the dangers of terminal uniqueness, why it's crucial to measure how employees (leaders included) feel about their work, supervisor, and organization, and why spending resources on leadership training is not only a "must have," but a reflection of organizational values. I also learned that top leaders, especially the CEO, must not be distant from the organization. Sure, Herb Kelleher had to deal with financing, Wall Street, and politics, but do not think for a minute that he was not engaged in operations. Other insights were that the quickest way to failure is for a CEO or top leader not to be engaged in operations, and that the best part of the job was getting to know the workforce.

Yes, it was painful for me to realize I was not the leader I had thought I was. It was ego deflating to go to Southwest and ask for help. I also had to go back to the employees and let them know I was wrong about it being easy to create a great customer experience. If the boss does not listen, if people don't have the resources to do the job, if goals aren't clear, if teamwork is lacking, if there's no feedback or positive recognition, it is very hard to do a good job. Yes, it was scary saying, "I work for you. What should I be doing today?" But it was a question worth asking.

We talk more about the basics of employee engagement throughout this book. But positive change begins with measurement.

Once you know the metrics in both areas—employee engagement and customer satisfaction—you can take steps to improve both. A few tips:

First, measure customer satisfaction. Not only will measuring help you know where you stand with customers, you'll end up with metrics that you can build a service goal around. It's not enough to just say "We want to improve customer satisfaction" or "We want a better customer experience." Most people are motivated by clarity and specificity, not vagueness. Plus, without a number, how will you know whether you have improved?

There are many tools for measuring customer satisfaction. The first step is to teach staff how to ask specific questions. This way, items can be addressed immediately. However, it is always good to also measure via a formal feedback system.

Next, measure employee engagement. Use an outside company that has expertise and experience in surveying. The company I have used for more than two decades uses a 47-question survey. Here are some of the types of questions it includes:

- I am kept informed on matters that affect me.
- I feel comfortable making suggestions to my supervisor.
- I feel safe at work.
- Employees are treated fairly here.
- The organization's leaders model ethical behavior.
- The organization is effective in retaining valuable employees.
- I am encouraged by the direction of the organization.
- The organization is dedicated to the satisfaction of its customers.

Those are just a few examples. The questions cover all aspects of a person's on-the-job experience, and categories cover the range of what is important to the workforce.

Take time to explain to all employees that their answers will be confidential. This will make it more likely they'll answer truthfully. Bigger than that, though, make sure you're taking steps to create a psychologically safe workplace. (See Chapter 21.) This will make it more likely that people will come to you with issues even without a survey.

Be ready to act when the results come in. Employees at first may doubt the survey results will be used so they will be pleasantly surprised by follow-through. Train all people in supervisory positions on how to share the data and create action plans. Keep the action plans in front of everyone. Make sure everyone knows they are a priority.

Identify those leaders who have the most engaged staff and learn what they do. Share those learnings with all people in supervisory positions. It starts at the top, with the CEO/top leader rolling out to their direct reports as well as a summary to all staff with the steps that will be followed by each supervisor.

Measure employee engagement as often as you can. This is a matter of preference. Companies used to measure engagement once a year, but many have moved to every six months or even more frequently. My feeling is that it's impossible to be too connected to how employees feel about their work. Between one larger survey and the next, it's a good idea to do a short one with fewer questions to assess concerns and to see if progress is being made.

Too many companies know their cash position way better than how their employees are doing. Ironically, the better the employees feel, the better cash position there is. The good news is that once the survey has been done and rolled out properly and actions have been taken, leaders cannot imagine *not* doing one.

Don't wait for the perfect time to measure how the workforce feels. Run to measurement, not from it. You will end up with a more engaged workforce, better customer satisfaction, and better financial performance.

We live in an age when it's no longer enough to get the core competencies right. We have to get a lot of other things right, too. Standards are higher than they've ever been, which means we have to always be improving. Measurement lets us know where we are *now*—and only when we know where we are now can we know where we want to be in the future.

40

Put a Well-Run Meeting System in Place:

Why a Large-Group/Small-Group Approach Often Works Best

People want to be included in decision making and have influence, which is a good sign. It shows they are engaged and feel a sense of ownership regarding the company's success.

And, of course, leaders want employees to feel included. There are so many benefits of having a good cross-section of people involved. For example, more and different ideas and perspectives come from larger groups. It can also create more buy-in on actions taken.

The same is true in a community. It's great when lots of citizens are very engaged and want to provide input into actions they feel will make the community better. Often, when I work with communities there are big groups of people working together on projects.

Yet even the best of things can have unintended consequences. As wonderful as it is having big groups of passionate people working together, there can also be challenges. For example, it is often very hard with a large group to get the scope of work to a doable point and to decide upon and prioritize actions. As a result, very little gets accomplished.

So is the answer always smaller groups? Jeff Bezos, founder and CEO of Amazon, famously talked about his two-pizza rule. By this he meant that if two pizzas can't feed the team, then the team is too big to be effective. Over the years, I have heard many suggestions on the optimal size of a group, team, and/or board. The size usually suggested is 5 to 12 people.

Yes, there are definitely some advantages to small groups and we'll talk more about them shortly. But what if you have a larger organization? What should you do if you want lots of input yet also want to make sure something gets accomplished quickly? Here is an example from my own experience that should work for you and meet your goals of input and perspectives as well as scope and priorities.

I was asked by a county to come discuss how to create a vibrant community. Prior to my arrival, the local newspaper conducted a survey of community members. On Day One, I met with a large group of these residents to share the results and then break into groups. For example, one group focused on what events could be held. Another group focused on what might increase shopping downtown. Yet another group focused on what could be done to get young people to stay in the community (among other topics). While no decisions were made on scope or priorities, there was a lot of input and many different perspectives were given.

Day Two was not intended to be a whole day but rather a scheduled two-hour session. To prepare for it, we reviewed Day One material. We were able to group the most pressing issues into about seven actions.

It had been decided that only a few representatives from each Day One group would attend this two-hour session. Thus, there were many fewer people on Day Two. The smaller group reviewed the summary and the seven items. They gave more thought to priorities. And they quickly narrowed the scope to three actions that could be accomplished over the next 90 days and settled on a communication plan for the Day One attendees and the community at large.

In other words, more decisions were made in two hours of Day Two than in eight hours of Day One. Does that mean Day Two was a better day?

Of course not! Day Two went so well due to the hard work of many on Day One. If only a small group met both days, we would have missed lots of ideas and perspectives. These made it possible to provide a summary for the Day Two session. If a large group had met on both days, I doubt we would have gotten to three action items in two hours of Day Two.

This approach to meetings captures the best of both worlds. If you want to try it inside your own company, here are a few tips that may help:

Trust the process. What seems like a few ideas will expand to the point that it will feel like little will be accomplished. However, as time goes by, the scope of what needs to be done narrows. It is a "narrow, wide, narrow" process. Don't panic midway through the big group day.

Before going to the small group, prepare a summary of Day One actions. Still more culling will be needed but this is a starting point.

Because the group is smaller on Day Two, let them prioritize the next steps. Ask them to narrow down the results from Day One into three action items. A nominal voting process works well.

Explain that just because an item did not make the top three does not mean it will be missed. It is about sequencing. By taking on fewer action items, I find more gets completed, not less, which builds trust and confidence. Then bring the group back to select the next items or to find a way to make the first three even better.

Create the communication plan and assign responsibilities. After completing the actions prescribed in Tip 4 it is easy to feel good and leave the session. Don't. Take time to create who will own each action and develop a communication plan to loop in the larger group who attended on Day One and any others who need to be communicated with.

Again, this strategy works well if you have a large company, organization, or community. There are certain facilitation skills that are needed to get the most out of large-group work as well as small-group work. Let's address large groups first:

How to Facilitate Large-Group Meetings

Before the meeting, get really clear on what you want to get done. In putting together an agenda, you might want to survey people before the meeting to get their idea. Or maybe do an assessment to identify problem areas or what they want to leave with. Share results at the beginning of the session or before the session is held. This way people will have a chance to get their best ideas out and process others' ideas. (This is especially helpful for introverts, who may not speak up if they don't have a chance to think things through ahead of time.)

Go over "housekeeping" rules up front. Let them know what to expect (when breaks will happen and so forth). Narrate that staying on schedule is important and thank them for their time. Don't just say, "We are going to take a 15-minute break." Tell them exactly what time to be back (i.e., say, "Be back at 10:15"). Have someone who can help get people back to their seats on time after breaks.

Ask people to be aware of communication styles (their own and others'). Remind people to be mindful of different styles so everyone has a chance to be heard. Ask them to focus on what they are saying and how they are saying it. Content does not trump communication. To involve those who are less assertive or shy, or who can't speak up quickly enough, simply ask their opinion—but let them know it's okay to take time to think about their answers first.

Room set-up matters. Round tables of six work nicely. Or, arrange seating in a U-shape. You want people up close where you can easily engage with them, so force them to the front. One way to do this is to place "reserved" signs on back chairs.

Job 1 is building a sense of community in the room. If you want people to contribute, it's important to put them at ease. Especially if most people in the group don't know one another, it's your job as the leader to establish a comfortable atmosphere and set the tone for the discussion.

Do table activities early in the meeting. A great table activity is asking for one question per table. Each table writes what question they have, and these are collected at the break. Collect the questions even from the tables that do not get called on.

Don't think of it as running a meeting but as facilitating a discussion. This means paying very close attention to what's happening in the room. Recently, I was facilitating a large group discussion and I quickly realized that while I came there to teach, what I really needed to be doing was building bridges and connecting the people in the room in a way that builds relationships. They needed to work together after I was gone to make anything work.

Know who is in the room. Try to get a list of who is attending and a little about them. This allows you to say more personal things and connect a few people in order to build social capital. If time allows, get people to introduce themselves.

Build in interaction. It won't happen on its own. This way, everyone can learn from the different perspectives, experiences, and ideas of the participants. Sometimes it's hard to get high levels of participation. Only a few (the "big mouths") really end up participating. Breakout sessions are great for sparking interaction. Give really clear instructions on the exercises. Consider putting them on a handout so the group can see them in writing. Assign a person in each group to report back.

Ask great questions, even if you know the answer. It's better if the ideas come from the group, even if you are the expert.

Look for ways to keep people engaged. For example, ask people their names and pull them into the examples. Have fun stories ready to recapture their interest.

Anticipate getting stuck on things and prepare some pivots for when things get stuck. I was in a neighborhood meeting where things weren't moving forward. I asked them to tell me what was good about their community (bright spots), and the whole meeting turned around.

Big groups can be incredibly valuable in moving your organization forward. It's a gift to have access to so many minds and voices. Be sure to use it to the fullest advantage.

How to Get the Most Out of Small-Group Meetings

Whether you work for a large organization following the "large-group/small-group" approach discussed at the start of this chapter, or a small business that by necessity has smaller, tight-knit teams, you need to know how to facilitate small groups. Before we get into the "how-tos," let's take a look at the many, many benefits of working with smaller groups:

Smaller groups move at a faster pace. This is partly a matter of logistics. It's easier to get five people together in one place than 15 people. Also, there are fewer people to weigh in, fewer viewpoints to consider, fewer arguments to be had.

They're better at getting specialized. In today's economy, it's not necessary to know a little about a lot of things. We have the internet for that. Far better to know a lot about one area. The fewer people there are, the quicker they all come to understand the task at hand. The more they understand about a subject and its challenges, the less likely they are to make costly mistakes.

People are highly engaged and motivated. The smaller the group is, the more likely individuals are to feel that their efforts are important and the more effort they will put forth. This makes smaller groups more entrepreneurial by nature.

High performers are more likely to be noticed. Individuals are more exposed in a small group. When you do a good job, your boss will see it, and you're more likely to be recognized and rewarded for it, which is great for morale.

It's easier to build trust and unity. The fewer people there are, the easier it is for them to get to know each other. The better they know each other, the more comfortable they are collaborating and sharing their ideas. They grow to trust each other more and they bond more deeply. This unity means individuals on small teams are more likely to work late together to shore up a project they're working on, or to go the extra mile to help a teammate.

Team members naturally coach and mentor each other. I'm a big believer in the value of mentoring. It not only strengthens a business but a community. In small teams, this kind of relationship occurs organically as people work together on the project at hand. More experienced people enjoy sharing their skills with less experienced people, and new employees appreciate the personal attention.

Be sure to choose smart, hardworking, and passionate people for your small team. That's important. But being a good facilitator may matter just as much. Your team may be overflowing with great ideas and raw energy, but without a good facilitator to bring them out, capture them, and direct them into the right channels, all that potential is lost.

A Few Tips for Facilitating a Great Small-Group Meeting

Show up armed with great questions. The key to a productive discussion is asking the right questions, so come to the meeting well prepared. (Open-ended questions are best.) We've all left a meeting and then realized, too late, that we forgot to address a critical issue.

When we do our homework on the front end, we minimize the chances of making this mistake.

Create the right environment. Seating should be arranged so people can easily see each other and make eye contact. Often a circle where everyone is at the same level and not too far apart works best. People need to be physically comfortable before they can be emotionally comfortable enough to be good collaborators.

Ask people to introduce themselves to the group. If everyone doesn't already know one another, go around the room and have each person talk about their role. People are more likely to communicate and build strong relationships when there's a good foundation from the start.

Dig deeper into people's answers with follow-up questions. Avoid asking yes/no questions or those that can be answered too simply. You want to dig deeper. When someone gives what seems to be a surface-level answer, don't let them off the hook. Ask, "Why do you think that?" or, "Let's say we go with that solution. How do you think customers might react?"

Be inclusive. If you're not careful, a few extroverts will take over the meeting. Quieter people may have great ideas but get drowned out by louder voices. You might call out introverts specifically, so they'll have a chance to contribute. (Just be sure they have the option to think about their answer and circle back to it later. Introverts often dislike being put on the spot.)

Keep the meeting on track. This requires that you have clear expectations around what you're trying to accomplish and that you communicate them with the team. If someone goes off on a tangent, make sure to steer them back quickly to the subject at hand. Similarly, discourage side discussions: everyone needs to be focused on the same talking points.

"Weight" discussion time in a way that matches the importance of the topic. You have limited time. Don't let a B or C item take up time that should be devoted to A items.

Get to solutions as quickly as possible. It's easy to stay focused on the problem and have everyone explain their version but try to use the bulk of the time to focus on solving the problems, not just discussing them. Breakout sessions (dividing up into smaller groups tasked with coming back with answers) are a great way to move the needle on this.

End the meeting with a clear action plan or at least some solid next steps. Remember, smaller groups can move things along more quickly so make sure everyone is well prepared to make that happen.

Life and business almost always reward action. The best teams are those that avoid "analysis paralysis" and show a strong bias toward rapid (though not rash) execution. When you keep this in mind at every step of the process, you'll be more likely to get the most value from your teams, no matter what the size.

41

Focus on What *Right* Looks Like:

How to Collect and Move Best Practices

What does *right* look like? While the question seems easy enough, the answer is often missed. All too often our human nature is to focus on what is wrong to the exclusion of what is right. Some years ago, I spoke at a Carnegie education conference. One of the featured presenters was Chip Heath. He and his brother, Dan, are noted authors. This was right after their book *Switch*, that spent 10 weeks on the *New York Times* bestseller list, had come out. In his presentation, Chip shared that a key to achieving better results is to spend more time on what is right versus what is wrong.

One example he used is that in studies of high school graduation rates, a tendency is to spend most of the time researching the children who drop out, not the ones who don't. He shared that yes, more children in poverty drop out than those children who are not in poverty. So, study the children who live in poverty who stay in school. Find out what's different about them and how it can be duplicated in others.

This rang a bell. Years ago, I was in a leadership role at Holy Cross Hospital in Chicago, and we had very low patient satisfaction. Of course, we came up with all sorts of reasons why our patient satisfaction was low, and most were things we felt we could not control. We let ourselves off the hook. Then one day we noticed one patient care unit had much higher patient satisfaction than anyplace else in the hospital. So we studied the manager of that unit, a woman named Michelle.

We noticed that Michelle started each day by going into every patient room. She made sure everything was good. She came out of the rooms and complimented the staff on what she heard that was positive and coached staff when things could be better. We said to her, "We notice you visit every patient every day." She replied, "Doesn't everyone?" The answer was no. After learning from Michelle, we had her teach all managers how to visit (round) on all patients. Soon we had some of the best patient satisfaction in the country.

Since then, I have found we leaders are much better off looking for and learning from what's right rather than just what is wrong. This approach has many benefits. It helps us learn what drives success as well as taking away excuses.

Also, it's far more efficient to benchmark techniques and processes that have been proven to work than struggling to reinvent the wheel. Back in 2010 I read an article in the *Harvard Business Review*, written by Oded Shenkar, on why imitation is a better business practice than innovation. The article made the point that "97.8 percent of the value of innovations goes to imitators."[1] It just makes good sense to find and imitate what's working well inside your own company.

A few years back I was asked to speak at an organization's sales team meeting. They had a goal to increase sales. So I started the meeting by asking the vice president of sales to point out the best of the 20 or so salespeople in the room. He quickly zeroed in on two people. I then spent time asking them several questions. Soon other salespeople did, too.

Often the answers are right in the room. Yet leaders can face a number of challenges in identifying best practices and applying them to other areas of the business.

One challenge, as I've already mentioned, is that we tend to automatically focus on who is not doing well. This is a fundamental mindset shift that needs to happen before we can move forward.

A second challenge is that we allow barriers like ego or fear to stand in the way. Our ego often stops us from asking for help. Along the same lines, fear—whether it's fear of being uncomfortable or fear of not being able to execute—has the same effect. I have found that senior leaders in particular face this challenge.

Third, we tend to relate more than compare. We think that what works for one division won't work for another. Perhaps we rationalize that the other division has better customers, better employees, a more ideal location, and so on. This is what I call "terminal uniqueness," and it's an attitude that will prevent you from improving and growing. Yes, there are always differences, but there are more commonalities.

The key is to take time to observe until you see what is either being done differently, more consistently, or more skillfully.

Finally, most employees don't get to observe the more successful people in their organization. I've spoken to educational leaders on occasion and I always note that most teachers rarely get to observe other teachers. This is true in many work areas. So, as a leader, it is imperative to study the bright spots, learn from them, and then scale them throughout the organization.

Here are some tips for finding and moving those bright spots (best practices):

Talk to your high performers—or customers of your high performers—to figure out what's going right. You will probably have to dig deep to find out what the superstars are doing differently from others. Sometimes it's a small nuance.

Once you've isolated the best practice, give some thought to how to transfer it. What outcomes do you want? Can you back up your desire for people to change with metrics? (Specificity tends to be more convincing than vagueness/generality.) What processes will help you move the practice? What training needs to happen? Can the high performer take on a teaching or coaching role to help colleagues and coworkers embrace the practice?

Expect some pushback. Sometimes the person who originated the best practice may be reluctant to share it. Sometimes others in the company don't want to change how they do things because their egos get in the way (or just because people naturally resist change). Other times people believe they are "terminally unique," and this new way of doing things won't work for them. In this last case, I find that often a slightly modified version of the best practice will work. Relate; don't compare.

Connect employees to the *why*. For example, you might say: "On our last customer satisfaction survey, customers said when we do it this way it makes their lives easier" or "This process consistently generates 30 percent more revenue for Jill's department" or "When Bob did it this way last quarter, he cut expenses by 19 percent." Often knowing the *why* behind what you're asking people to do is enough to push them through their discomfort enough to change the way they do their job.

Make the change a requirement, not a suggestion. Hold people accountable for results. This will greatly increase the likelihood that they put the new behavior into practice.

If someone isn't mastering the new practice, determine if it's a will or skill issue. Then deal with it accordingly. Generally, skill can be taught if the will is there. If the will isn't there, it might be time to make some tough decisions.

Reward and recognize those who stand out. What gets rewarded gets repeated. Public praise or even a small reward like a gift card to a local restaurant or movie theater go a long way. When others see those who adopt new behaviors being rewarded, they'll want in on the action, too.

Teach everyone to look for best practices and bright spots. It's not just a job for leaders. Often frontline people are more in touch with what's working well. Make it clear that you want people never to stop searching for ways to do their job better.

As leaders, we set the tone for culture. We need to get in the habit of focusing on what's going right, leveraging it, and looking for ways to do things even better. When we do this consistently, others "catch" our attitude and emulate it. Over time, this can spark a powerful turn-around for a company.

Note

1. Oded Shenkar, "Defend Your Research: Imitation Is More Valuable Than Innovation," *Harvard Business Review*, April 2010, https://hbr .org/2010/04/defend-your-research-imitation-is-more-valuable-than -innovation.

A Final Thought: Putting It All into Practice

Now that you have read this book, it's time to implement what you've learned. It's time to ask yourself, "What am I going to do differently now? How can I use what I have learned to change my behavior for the better and encourage others in the company to change theirs as well?"

My suggestion is to take a few chapters at a time and work to get those tactics right before you move on to something else. Trying to do everything at once is too overwhelming. Once you've made some headway you'll get a boost of enthusiasm and energy that will power you to tackle the next areas.

This book can serve as an on-boarding tool for new leaders at all levels. When they read it up front they'll be able to start their career with your company on the right foot. Current leaders may also read it as a refresher course. Even when we're not actively working to change some aspect of how we lead, it's good to always keep the principles of great leadership at the top of our minds.

Don't expect to master the concepts in this book overnight. Improving our leadership is a gradual process. Be kind to yourself and others inside your company who are working to get better and better. Nothing worth doing is easy or quick. Leadership is both an art and a science and as such requires time, repetition, and patience.

Most of all, I hope you learn something new from reading this book. I learned a lot from writing it. Being a great leader is no different from being a great employee or a great human being: we never, ever stop learning.

Thank you for reading *The Busy Leader's Handbook*. I am grateful for having the opportunity to play a small role in your leadership journey.

Quint Studer

Acknowledgments

Norm Adams was a wonderful friend and mentor to many. Years ago, I was thanking him for being such a great help to me. When I was done, he looked at me and said, "One area we may never agree on is who is helping who more." His message was that somehow his taking time to guide and teach me was helping him as much or more as it helped me. Today, some 20 years later, I understand to the core of my soul what he meant.

I was once asked in an interview to talk about a turning point in my own career. As with most people, there are many turning points. The one I shared was watching the video *In Search of Excellence*, then reading the book of the same title by Thomas J. Peters and Robert H. Waterman. At the time I was a new supervisor and I felt totally unprepared. I was too afraid to share with others how "in over my head" I felt. The local library in Janesville, Wisconsin, was showing a film of Tom Peters talking about excellence, so I went. While I knew I still had a long way to go, the film and then the book provided me the hope that maybe I could do this leadership thing.

I hope this book will do the same for others, that it provides them with new skills, reinforces what is already being done, and/or provides adjustments to actions to make leadership more effective and rewarding.

A name could be put on each chapter of a person and an organization that brought about the learnings. At times these tips were developed in a work session with a group of managers on how to best handle a situation. Then, due to my travels and working with more organizations and communities, these tools and techniques were refined, retested, and when it became apparent that they worked, shared with other people, organizations, and communities.

However, in writing the book, I've included some very new tips and techniques as well as further enhancements of some tried and true methods to create great companies and communities.

With my other books, by the time they are complete the feeling of crossing the finish line is there; thus, my acknowledgments have been on the short side. This time, while the finish line feels the same, writing a book that covers decades of life and work brings to light the many people and places I am grateful to—so please bear with me if the list is a little longer.

To all those individuals and groups I have worked with for so many years, thank you. As Norm said, you have helped me more than I have helped you.

To my father, Quinton, and mother, Shirley, my deepest thanks for creating in me a strong work ethic and a willingness to challenge myself and the status quo.

I would like to thank my wife, Rishy, who has been a constant supporter and mirror to me. Just the other night I shared with her that someone said I was a bit of a challenge. With a smile, she said, "No! Really?" Her belief in me and her willingness to raise children while I traveled, as well as her constant work in her own businesses, sets the tone for what a mature adult does. This is a journey I am still on.

To my children and grandchildren, I hope you think of me as I do my own parents and grandparents.

I would also like to extend my most heartfelt gratitude to the following people and places:

To Miss James, Mr. Fry, and Coach King, three key teachers who made such an impact on me that decades later my gratitude only increases.

To the University of Wisconsin–Whitewater, which accepted me on probation, was always there to be helpful, and remains an important part of my life today.

To the School District of Janesville, Wisconsin, and Cooperate Education Service Agency (CESA) 17 (now CESA 2), which provided learning opportunities in being useful to others and provided me with examples of what right looks like.

To Parkside Lodge of Wisconsin, a small drug and alcoholism treatment center that hired me as a community relations representative, and that allowed me to still work with school districts and introduced me to healthcare and small businesses.

To Mercy Health System, Janesville, Wisconsin, which stretched me and taught me about seeing big goals.

To Holy Cross Hospital in Chicago. This is where CEO Mark Clement showed me how investing in leadership training and setting clear goals works.

To Baptist Hospital in Pensacola, Florida, for giving me the opportunity to be president. What a great hospital and what a great learning experience. I will always be grateful for their support as I started Studer Group.

To the many staff who made Studer Group a special place. My time until I sold the company was filled with great people both internally and those affiliated with the great organization we worked with.

To the many wonderful people I work with today, from the minor league baseball team the Pensacola Blue Wahoos to the places in our community where people eat, live, learn, and play: what role models in difference-making you are.

To the board and staff of the Studer Community Institute: thank you for the work being done in early brain development, in skill building for those hard-working small and mid-size business owners and managers, and in the arena of civic engagement.

To Lisa Nellessen-Savage and the *Pensacola News Journal*, who each Sunday runs my column on leadership. Thank you for keeping the *News Journal* a difference-making paper and for making sure local news stays in the forefront. You are everything a leader needs to be.

To Barbara Scott Payne (my "wing person") and Nicole Webb Bodie. Both have played instrumental roles in getting my new venture, Vibrant Community Partners—a company that is based on my book *Building a Vibrant Community*—off the ground. We work with communities to help them keep talent at home, attract talent back, and improve the quality of life for residents. Also, a big shout-out to Anna White for all her hard work on VCP before going off to law school.

To Matt Holt of John Wiley & Sons. Matt sets the example of bringing information to readers that will help them, their businesses, and the community.

To Dottie DeHart, my partner in building Vibrant Community Partners. Dottie is my coach, mentor, and a person who pushes one beyond what they feel they can do. I met her more than a decade ago when Wiley asked her to assist me with my book *Results That Last*. Since then we have been together with each book and most importantly, we share a passion and desire to make a difference. This book, like my others, would not have happened without Dottie. I am grateful for and to her.

And, as always, thank you to all the friends of Bill W.

I have been blessed beyond measure to know all of these wonderful people. Thank you all for being a part of my journey.

About the Author

Quint Studer is a lifelong student of leadership. He is a businessman, a visionary, an entrepreneur, and a mentor to many. He has worked with individuals at all levels of leadership and across a variety of industries to help them become better leaders and create high-performing organizations. Along the way he has discovered and refined many high-impact leadership behaviors and tactics that he is eager to share. Some of the most powerful are found in this book.

He knows leadership is not easy and wants to simplify it for others. He has a gift for translating complex business strategies into simple, doable leader behaviors that allow organizations to achieve long-term success and profitability.

Quint is a teacher at heart. In fact, he began his leadership journey working with special needs children—a job he loved and held for 10 years. He entered the healthcare industry in 1984 as a Community Relations Representative. He then went on to hold leadership positions at Mercy Health System in Wisconsin and Holy Cross Hospital in Chicago, Illinois, where their initiatives in patient care led to their winning Hospitals Magazine's Great Comeback award. In 1996, he became president of Baptist Hospital in Pensacola, Florida, leading that organization to the top 1 percent of hospitals nationwide in patient and employee satisfaction.

In 2000, after numerous requests by organizations for assistance, Studer Group was formed. Over the years the outcomes firm won multiple awards, including the 2010 Malcolm Baldrige National Quality Award. By the time the firm was sold in 2015, it had 250 employees and had helped more than a thousand healthcare organizations move toward higher performance.

Through his work at Studer Group, he served as a role model for hundreds of CEOs and other administrative leaders around the country. During this time, he was honored to receive several accolades for his leadership. *Inc.* magazine named Studer its Master of Business, making him the only healthcare leader to have ever won this award. *Modern Healthcare* has chosen him twice as one of the 100 Most Powerful People in Healthcare for his work on institutional healthcare improvement. *Modern Healthcare*, along with its sister publication *Advertising Age*, also honored him with the first Healthcare Marketing Visionary IMPACT award in 2014. Around the same time *Becker's Hospital Review* recognized him as one of the 40 smartest people in healthcare.

Quint made a lasting contribution to healthcare by connecting patient care to the concept of customer service. Sunrise Hospital and Medical Center Vice President of Patent Experience Cyndi Tierney was quoted as saying that Quint put patient experience "on the map."

In his travels throughout the United States, Quint witnessed significant differences in the vitality of the communities he visited. Some were doing well, and others not as well. His observations on what made the difference—along with research he read on why communities thrive—inspired him to help make his home community of Pensacola a haven for small businesses.

In 2015 he sold Studer Group to focus on channeling his passion for leadership into community development. As the founder of Studer Community Institute, he has been integral in revitalizing Pensacola, which has seen 34 percent growth in property values in the past five years and has won several awards for its thriving downtown. He captured this story in his 2018 book, *Building a Vibrant Community: How Citizen-Powered Change Is Reshaping America.*

Most recently, Pensacola won the 2019 Strongest Town Contest hosted by nonprofit organization Strong Towns. The competition is designed to spotlight communities from around the world that are building enduring financial resilience at the local level and actively embodying the Strong Towns approach to economic growth and development.

A core part of Quint's strategy centers on leadership skills training for entrepreneurs and small business leaders. SCI holds training and development workshops and small business roundtables every month. It also hosts EntreCon, a conference held in Pensacola each November just for entrepreneurs.

His newest venture is Vibrant Community Partners, a company that coaches communities in building out a blueprint for achieving growth and excellence. The firm focuses on education, downtown development, and economic development, including training for small businesses and civic engagement.

Quint has a great love for teaching his leadership insights in books: he has authored eight of them in addition to *The Busy Leader's Handbook*. His *Results That Last* reached number seven on the *Wall Street Journal*'s bestseller list of business books. In *The Great Employee Handbook* he shares insights from working with thousands of employees during his career.

He has spoken to a wide range of audiences across the United States, and is a nationally recognized expert regarding leadership. He is often interviewed by radio and TV shows, as well as magazines and newspapers across the country.

Quint was named in *Florida Trend*'s 500 Most Influential Business Leaders list for 2018. He currently serves as the Entrepreneur-in-Residence at the University of West Florida, which in 2018 named him an Honorary Doctor of Letters.

He and his wife, Rishy, are residents of Pensacola, Florida. Passionate about giving back to the community, they share their time and resources with local and national nonprofit organizations.

To learn more, please visit www.thebusyleadershandbook.com, www.studeri.org, and www.vibrantcommunityblueprint.com.

Index

HOW QUINT STUDER CAN HELP YOUR ORGANIZATION. . . AND YOUR COMMUNITY

The Busy Leader's Handbook is more than a book. It's a blueprint for transforming organizations of all shapes and sizes. It's also a springboard for communities that want to strengthen and galvanize their local business presence as they move toward vibrancy.

Quint Studer, the author of *The Busy Leader's Handbook*, is also a master speaker and consultant with decades of experience in helping people. Like many leaders, Quint has learned as his career progressed. He has gone from serving as president of a 1,700-employee organization to starting, building, and selling a company to now owning a number of small businesses, including a Double-A minor league baseball team. Along the way, he has picked up methods and insights from the many leaders he has worked with. Today, his Studer Community Institute (SCI) provides skill-building for managers and people in other leadership positions.

This book brings together much of what Quint learned throughout his career in business and as a community leader. He brings these lessons to life by helping you focus on the fundamentals of leadership and apply them to your own organization. Whether you're a business owner or a community leader, you can engage Quint to help you in a variety of capacities:

For Organizations. . . ━━━━━━━━━━

Book Quint for a leadership workshop or engage him to speak to your business or organization. He will share proven best practices, tools, tips, and tactics for engaging employees, delighting customers, and sustaining high performance. You'll be able to take what you learn and put it into practice right away.

Quint will help you:

- Get your organization back to basics and reinforce the leadership skills and behaviors that lead to consistently high organizational performance
- Move your middle management team to a higher level of effectiveness (this is the group that makes or breaks your company)
- Get everyone in your company aligned and singing from the same hymnal
- Create and sustain a culture that keeps employees engaged and motivated and attracts and retains high performers
- Hire the right people, onboard them in a way that immediately gets them on the right path, and optimize their performance over time
- Put the right processes, practices, and other foundational structures in place early on so that you create clarity and head off problems before they derail you

For Communities. . .

Quint is in the business of helping communities revitalize themselves. His book *Building a Vibrant Community: How Citizen-Powered Change Is Reshaping America* provides a blueprint for community leaders and shares the story of Pensacola, Florida's revitalization. (Visit www.vibrantcommunityblueprint.com to learn more.)

In the last four of five years, Pensacola has improved its assessed property value over 30 percent, has gotten investments in the downtown community up 60 percent, and has seen the population grow by 5.4 percent after years of decline. And a big part of its success has to do with its thriving and galvanized small business community and its well-trained business leaders.

Business owners are passionate about what they do; however, the skills needed to sustain a business are often not there. That's why Studer Community Institute (SCI) offers "roundtables" and monthly training and development sessions to Pensacola business owners. Live workshops, webinars, online content, and toolkits help them increase productivity, reduce turnover, promote business growth and job creation, and improve service. SCI also sponsors EntreCon, an annual conference focused on entrepreneurship and continued learning.

Training small business owners in the fundamentals of great leadership just makes sense for communities looking to become more vibrant. Successful business owners create jobs. They pay rent and taxes. They also give back to the community in other ways. Yet it's estimated that 40 percent of new businesses fail in their first year and that 80 percent don't make it five years. Strong, vibrant communities make it easy for new businesses to get started *and* help keep existing ones healthy long-term. They know transferring vital knowledge and experience to entrepreneurs is critical to everyone's success.

Quint can assist your community in developing the training and development infrastructure to help your small businesses thrive long-term.

You will learn:

- How to identify the leadership skills your community should focus on
- How to identify local talent to handle the teaching and coaching
- How to organize and market monthly training sessions and business roundtables
- How to set scheduling, pricing, and sponsors
- How to galvanize your small business community (and why you should)
- How to set up and run a small business challenge
- How to utilize resources such as monthly small business columns and EntreCon

The above items are just examples of what Quint can focus on in his presentations and workshops. He will gladly customize a session for your organization or community.

To learn more, please visit www.thebusyleadershandbook.com, www.studeri.org, and www.vibrantcommunityblueprint.com. To engage Quint for a speaking event or training workshop, please call Nicole Webb Bodie at 850-748-2027 or email nwebb@studeri.org.